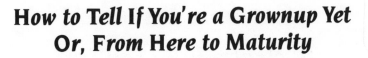

**How to Tell If You're a Grownup Yet
Or, From Here to Maturity**

**Cornelia Ravenal**

*illustrations by Ian Ross*

# HOW TO TELL IF YOU'RE A GROWNUP YET
## or,
## *from here to maturity*

COLLIER BOOKS

Macmillan Publishing Company

New York

MACMILLAN PUBLISHING COMPANY
866 Third Avenue, New York, N.Y. 10022
Collier Macmillan Canada, Inc.

Library of Congress Cataloging in Publication Data
Ravenal, Cornelia.
How to tell if you're a grownup yet, or, from here
to maturity.
1. Maturation (Psychology)—Anecdotes, facetiae,
satire, etc.  I. Title.  II. Title: From here to
maturity.
PN6231.M37R38  1985       155.6       84-29359
ISBN 0-02-081210-8

Macmillan books are available at special discounts
for bulk purchases for sales promotions, premiums,
fund-raising, or educational use. For details, contact:

Special Sales Director
Macmillan Publishing Company
866 Third Avenue
New York, New York 10022

10  9  8  7  6  5  4  3  2

Printed in the United States of America

Of late I appear
To have reached the stage
When people look old
Who are only my age.

— Richard Armour

You can tell you're a grown-up when...

OR

The difference between a grownup and a mere adult is...

(see p. 1)

# Contents

# ACKNOWLEDGMENTS

This book is dedicated to my father.

I would also like to thank the following people, without whom (as they say) this would never have been possible: Becca Ravenal, Stan Gruen, Harry Wiland, and my agent, Ron Bernstein.

I'd like to especially thank Linda Semans, whose help was invaluable.

# INTRODUCTION:
# From Here to Maturity

When you were a child, the world was divided into two groups: Children and Grownups. As you got older, people tried to make you behave, and clowns on the playground yelled "Aw, grow up!" but you never thought it could happen to you. Even when you found yourself voting, driving, or drinking a G&T, deep down you still thought of yourself as a child. Then, before you expected it, store clerks started calling you "Sir" or "Ma'am," and you heard sub-four-footers referring to you as "that lady," or "that man." Had you really grown up just like that?

Probably not. You may be over eighteen, but age alone does not a Grownup make. Without the proper attitude, an adult is a Mere Adult. A Mere Adult is anyone old enough to play the game. A Grownup is someone who knows all the rules.

If you came of age in the late seventies or early eighties, you probably think there aren't any rules. Maybe you make excuses, like "They changed so fast I couldn't keep up." Too bad. The Age of Adolescence is over. If you think "I'm O.K., you're O.K.," you're not. Immaturity is OUT. Grownup is IN.

But what *are* the rules? Here are some clues:

**YOU ARE A GROWNUP IF YOU...**

get an occasional parking ticket.

like Vincent van Gogh because of his manic style.

wear clean underwear.

send out all your shirts.

**A MERE ADULT IF YOU...**

brag about how many you have.

really like him because his colors are bright.

wear underwear with holes.

leave them in a pile for weeks.

**A LOST CAUSE IF YOU...**

brag about how many you haven't paid.

like him even more because he cut off his ear.

wear anything edible.

jump around in them as if they're a pile of leaves.

Yes

Maybe

Forget It

| YOU ARE A GROWNUP IF YOU… | A MERE ADULT IF YOU… | A LOST CAUSE IF YOU… |
|---|---|---|
| have Librium, Excedrin, and Rolaids in your medicine cabinet. | have to mash pills into food to get them down. | take anything that looks good. |
| pay your phone bill before it's due. | leave it in the mailbox for a couple of days. | leave it in the mailbox and hope it goes away. |
| know everybody's birthday. | know everybody's sign. | know how many times you've "scored." |
| have a secretary who screens your calls. | don't get enough calls to screen. | pretend *you're* a secretary so you can screen your calls. |
| call your parents twice a month. | go home twice a month. | live at home. |
| are honest with yourself. | are honest only with yourself. | don't think you have to be honest with anybody. |

Sounds grim, doesn't it? But being a Grownup isn't all tax forms and responsibility. You get better dates if you're a Grownup. Better jobs. Better sex. Real estate. Life is better if you're a Grownup, or at least if you know how to fool everyone else into thinking you are.

After reading the essays, essaying the quizzes, digesting the quotes, perusing the lists, memorizing the vocabulary, and studying the illustrations with all the concentration they deserve, you may still have some profound philosophical and psychological questions about the nature of Grownupness. This book will answer none of them.

What How to Tell If You're a Grownup Yet will do is tell you how far you've gotten, how far you have to go, and whether it's worth it to go all the way. Most important, it will give you a lot of faking techniques, which are a lot less trouble than actually growing up. After all, faking it is what it's all about.

# How Badly Do You Need This Book? The Quizzes

Use a number two pencil. Work as quickly as you can. There is no penalty for guessing.

## THE GROWNUP AT HOME

If the truth be known, you'd have to say that you live
(a) off your parents.
(b) in a pigsty.
(c) to boogie.
(d) very well, considering the cost of living these days.

To polish the furniture, you use
(a) Pledge.
(b) lemon oil.
(c) nothing. That's the great thing about orange crates —they don't need polishing.
(d) a maid.

Your living room furniture is covered by
(a) cat hairs.
(b) old newspapers.
(c) plastic slipcovers.
(d) *House Beautiful.*

Your favorite bedspread is
(a) a purple-and-maroon Indian number.
(b) the same one you had in college.
(c) on the floor, usually.
(d) in the guest room.

The most prominent thing on your refrigerator door is
(a) a *Doonesbury* cartoon.
(b) last year's Christie Brinkley calendar.
(c) cute little magnets.
(d) the handle.

Even when you're busy, you never run out of
(a) beer.
(b) rolling papers.
(c) cigarettes.
(d) toilet paper.

You would never dream of leaving
(a) a party early.
(b) anything for the last minute.
(c) more than a 15 percent tip.
(d) the toilet seat up.

## THE GROWNUP AT WORK

Which of the following songs best describes your job?
(a) "I Can't Get Started"
(b) "Workin' on the Chain Gang"
(c) "Take This Job and Shove It"
(d) "Eight Days a Week"

Your desk is covered with
(a) papers.
(b) fast food.
(c) cigarette burns.
(d) Formica.

You are out of work. You say you are
(a) looking for a job.
(b) registering your objection to the capitalist system.
(c) self-unemployed.
(d) between projects.

You do not get an award or promotion you've been expecting. You
(a) sulk.
(b) cry, and hope everyone sees you and feels guilty.
(c) congratulate the person who got it; wonder who the person slept with.
(d) congratulate the person who got it; wonder who *you* should sleep with.
(e) begin looking for a way out

The last time you were at a copy center, you copied
(a) a chain letter.
(b) your face.
(c) a paper clip, just to see how it would come out.
(d) nothing. When you need things copied, you send someone out.
(e) none of the above

When you leave the office, you bring home
(a) a headache.
(b) your secretary.
(c) notepads, paper clips...depends on the day.
(d) work.

## THE GROWNUP AT PLAY

After a hard day, you like to unwind with
(a) a joint.
(b) the boys.
(c) a blond.
(d) the network news.
(e) TV or ice cream or job

When you have a good time, you usually say,
(a) "It was awesome."
(b) "We're talkin' supergreat."
(c) "Like woah. Totally."
(d) "I had a good time."

How do you spell relief?
(a) R–O–L–A–I–D–S
(b) V–A–L–I–U–M
(c) S–L–E–E–P
(d) R–E–L–I–E–F

Your idea of a perfect Saturday morning is
(a) when you can remember what you did Friday night.
(b) when you *can't* remember what you did Friday night.
(c) one that starts at noon.
(d) one not spent on line at Sears.

You've decided to give a party. What do you say?
(a) "It starts around ten. And BYOB."
(b) "Wanna get wasted?"
(c) "My parents are out of town."
(d) "Why don't you come by for drinks? Say, about seven."

(a) Do you like Trivia Pursuit

Which of the following describes your sex life?
(a) "Strangers in the Night"
(b) "He's Got the Whole World in His Hands"
(c) "Silk Stockings"
(d) "Ain't Misbehavin'"

You wouldn't dream of going on vacation without
(a) suntan oil.
(b) a backpack.
(c) *Let's Go Europe*!
(d) having your mail held.

You won't go to the beach without
(a) oil.
(b) a blond.
(c) a ghetto blaster.
(d) going through customs.

When you want a lifeguard, you
(a) pick one with muscles.
(b) go for the blond.
(c) bat your lashes.
(d) are probably drowning.

Pick one thing you'd never say on the phone:
(a) "I'm going to put you on conference call, O.K.?"
(b) "Nice talking to you."
(c) "Let me get a pencil."
(d) "Do you have Prince Albert in a can?"

How do you get exactly what you want for Christmas?
(a) Write to Santa Claus.
(b) Talk in your sleep.

(c) Make sure your husband and children know the name, color, and serial number of the expected gift.

(d) Buy it.

## THE GROWNUP IN PUBLIC

When you're walking down the street in broad daylight, you are most worried about
(a) getting lost.
(b) getting mugged.
(c) being caught talking to yourself.
(d) how the market's doing.

At the supermarket checkout counter, you
(a) read the *Enquirer*.
(b) try to pick someone up.
(c) hide what you don't need in the magazine rack.
(d) make out a check.

You need change for a phone call. You run to the nearest cash register. The cashier won't give out change. You
(a) give her the finger.
(b) throw a fit.
(c) say, "Ohhhkay," and then nod at her as if you've just decided to take a contract out on her life.

(d) calmly remove a twenty-dollar bill from your wallet and buy a five-cent piece of gum.

Your most important source of information is
(a) Jeane Dixon.
(b) MTV.
(c) Dan Rather.
(d) the old boy network.

"Some of my best friends are
(a) a little strange."
(b) doing time."
(c) singing waiters."
(d) pregnant."

"Lots of people I know have
(a) pimples."
(b) drug problems."
(c) one-night stands."
(d) mortgages."

When you have a little extra cash, you buy
(a) Pez.  ?
(b) drugs.
(c) shoes.
(d) T-bills.
(e) books — like this one

Pick the word that doesn't belong:
(a) gross
(b) awesome
(c) nerdlike
(d) negotiable

Pick the phrase that doesn't belong:
(a) "Gross me out."
(b) "Woah like totally."
(c) "Where's the party?"
(d) "My secretary will get back to you."

You and the person closest to you have a falling out. You call
(a) your mother.
(b) your psychiatrist.
(c) someone you've always had a "thing" for.
(d) a lawyer.
(e) the bargain theatre to see what's playing

You usually eat in
(a) a high chair.
(b) McDonald's.
(c) restaurants that let you use Daddy's Amex.
(d) because it's cheaper than eating out.

8
E = 4 (5 if answer twice to same Q.)

## HOW TO SCORE

If you answered (a) to most of the questions:
9
Most of your friends are as immature as you are, but that's no excuse. Since you're a decade or more past the Wonder Years, maybe you'd better wonder what went wrong.

If you answered (b) to most of the questions:
0
You need this book more than anyone, but you'll undoubtedly miss most of the main points. That shouldn't deter you, however, from putting it by your bed. Or telling everyone that you read it.

If you answered (c) to most of the questions:
5
You are best described as "going through a stage." It could last a year, or it could last ten years, depending on how long it takes you to memorize the book.

If you answered (d) to most of the questions:
17
No question who's a Grownup here. Oh, yes, you know how to be sophisticated and mature. Now that you've mastered maturity, let's move on to the finer points.

If you changed your answers after reading the scoring system:
You're only fooling yourself. But since fooling people is an important part of Grownupness, that's O.K. You've got to start somewhere.

# GrownupSpeak

## Talking Like a Grownup: Introductory GrownupSpeak

Language is key in the creation of the Grownup image. You can get a job, wear a suit, and intimidate the hell out of little kids, but you'll blow the whole thing if you still talk like the Beaver. Words like *gosh* and *neat* made you sound like a dork when you were a teenager; over the age of twenty-one, they barely make you sound like a Mere Adult.

This is where GrownupSpeak comes in. Direct, yet understated, GrownupSpeak achieves its effect through consistently proper use of vocabulary, syntax, and diction (or at least reflects an effort to get them right). When a Grownup asks someone to accompany him or her to the cinema, he or she says, "Would you like to see a film tonight? We could go to the early show." A Grownup does not say, "Hey, wanna like catch a movie or sump'm? Maybe later, like if we're in the mood 'n' if we still feel like it?" This makes even the most imposing adult sound like he's wearing Clearasil.

GrownupSpeak is also a collection of buzz words. Like *eons* and *shelter* and *eye out*, which when used in the proper contexts, form Grownup-sounding sentences ranging from:

"I haven't seen you in eons!"

to

"Invest in real estate—it throws off shelter."

to

"You'll put your eye out!"

It's also using expressions of surprise and delight, like "Well, isn't that something?" and "How do you like that?" when a Mere Adult might say "Woahhhhhhhhhhhhhhhh!" or "How gross can you get?"

GrownupSpeak also addresses itself to the proper grownup usages of language. Children use language to get what they want. Mere Adults use language to call attention to themselves. Grownups use language to get what they want *without* calling attention to themselves. In keeping with this, Grownups don't think up cute nicknames for things that already have perfectly acceptable names. They understand that the object of language is to make themselves understood, not to make themselves annoying.

| GROWNUP TERMS | MERE ADULT TERMS |
| --- | --- |
| toddler | rug rat |
| parents | 'rents |
| car | wheels |
| record | tunes |
| party | bash |
| hairstyle | 'doo |
| drunk | looped |
| very drunk | ripped |
| extremely drunk | plastered to the wall |
| food | chow |
| good-bye | ciao |
| your mother | ciao mama |

---

**THOUGHT MOST COMMONLY EXPRESSED BY GROWNUPS TO CHILDREN**

"I thought I told you to go before we left the house."

**THOUGHT MOST COMMONLY EXPRESSED BY GROWNUPS TO GROWNUPS**

"I thought you were finished with it, so I threw it out."

---

Finally, GrownupSpeak is tact, or the art of offending no one by saying nothing.

=====

| WHAT YOU MEAN | WHAT YOU USED TO SAY | WHAT YOU SHOULD SAY |
|---|---|---|
| I have to go to the bathroom. | "Where's the can?" | "Excuse me for a moment. I'll be right back." |
| I never want to see you again. | "Bug off, buster." | "Let's have lunch." |
| Your cooking is inedible. | "I'm a vegetarian." | "I didn't know you could cook!" |
| That's a ridiculous idea. | "You're kidding, right?" | "Let me think about it...and I'll get back to you later in the week." |
| Your apartment is atrocious. | Nothing. | "Who's your decorator?" |
| Let's have sex. | "Let's get stoned." | "Can I freshen your drink?" |
| I hated the book. | "The pits. I'm using it to even out a table leg." | "Not bad for a first novel." |
| Maybe I'm stupid, but I didn't get that movie at all. | "I was so bored I fell asleep." | "I read the reviews. They were mixed." |
| Phone bill? What phone bill? | "I never got it. And I was wondering why it wasn't delivered this month." | "The check's in the mail." |
| I wish my mother would leave me alone. | "Mothurrrrrrrrrrrrrr!" | "I'm a grown adult. I can run my own life." |
| This party is so dull I'm going to go into a coma. | Nothing. You'd just leave. | "It's been a lovely evening, but I'm afraid we have to go." |

| WHAT YOU MEAN | WHAT YOU USED TO SAY | WHAT YOU SHOULD SAY |
|---|---|---|
| This date is so boring I'm going to go into a coma. | If you were on a date—nothing. You'd just go into the bathroom and pretend to be sick. | "Excuse me for a moment—I'll be right back." Maybe you will. |
| This bar is so dull I'm going to go into a coma. | Nothing. You'd just roll your eyes. | "Excuse me for a moment—I'll be right back." |

"Sure, I'll listen—I've got nowhere to go."

"Uh, yeah. Listen, I gotta make a phone call."

# *Excuses*

Everyone uses excuses, but Grownups don't have to use as many as Mere Adults because they are more responsible and, therefore, do not get into as many jams. When they do, however, they do not use an excuse that other Grownups can see through. They use an acceptable brush-off.

---

THE ACCEPTABLE BRUSH-OFF

"Listen, I'm running late. But it was nice talking to you."

"I'm making out a check right now."

"It's in the mail."

"Call my service. We'll have lunch."

"Sorry we're late. We ran into traffic."

THE EXCUSE THAT NEVER WORKS

"Oh no, I smell something burning on the stove, and uhm, gosh, I think I heard the door."

"It bounced? Oh no, Jeez, the bank must have made a mistake. I'm going to have to go in and yell at them."

"I swear I, like, mailed it yesterday. Or the day before. You know, the post office loses everything."

"I think I'm busy on Saturday. I have to, like, be out of town. There's a chance I won't be, but not a very big one."

"Sorry we're late. The phone rang *just* as we were leaving the house, and it turned out to be a friend of mine who *had* to talk to me for forty-five minutes, and then we got in the car and almost ran out of gas, so we had to stop at a gas station, where we got stuck in a line, and then the traffic! You wouldn't *believe* the traffic! Insane! Horrendous! I hope the dinner's not burned."

Finally, if you want to fool everyone into thinking you've left Mere Adulthood for good—especially on the phone when they can only hear your voice—forget the following words:

---

**WORDS TO FORGET (AS SOON AS POSSIBLE)**

van (unless followed by Heflin or preceded by
   Ludwig)
grind (unless giving a recipe)
freak out (either as a noun or a verb)
backpack (likewise)
gross (unless in opposition to *net*)
cool (unless in reference to the weather)
ridiculous (as in "That party was ridiculous.")
cruisin'
truckin'
serious (ridiculous, only more so)
stellar (very serious)
dummy (unless you play bridge)
mommy (being president is no excuse)
daddy (especially if preceded by sugar)
crummy, dopey, icky, lousy (all best replaced by
   *ill-advised*)

---

# Grownup Values

Grownups have values. Mere Adults have "attitudes." There are many differences between them. Values are held, usually deeply, and are a collection of ideals and principles that developed so that civilization could proceed. Attitudes, on the other hand, are "copped," usually for effect, and have nothing whatsoever to do with civilized behavior. They developed so that Mere Adults could be self-indulgent and show off. When values are translated into behavior, life runs more smoothly, because everybody knows what to expect. When attitudes are translated into behavior, the simplest transactions get complicated, because some Mere Adult is acting like the world revolves around him or her.

## The Big Five

1. Awareness (as opposed to "self-awareness")
2. Responsibility (as opposed to "winging it")
3. Discretion (as opposed to "asserting yourself")
4. Discipline (as opposed to "hanging out")
5. Patience (as opposed to "going for it")

More about these later. First, let's dispense with the biggest stumbling block facing any Mere Adult who is attempting to overcome his or her hopefully temporary state: Sophistication.

Sophistication is the attitude that Mere Adults cop when they want to appear grownup. It consists of behavior they used to think was grownup when they were children, like spending lots of money, blowing smoke rings, using a cigarette holder, and driving a Maserati. It often reflects an unfortunate obsession with Europe and manifests itself in an undue emphasis on knowing how to treat the servants, where the hot spots are on the Riviera, which wines to serve with which courses, and how to make it from New York to London to Rio for three parties on the same weekend.

Obviously, what Mere Adults think is sophistication is merely pretension. Grownups can be sophisticated, but not if they don't have the five real values down *cold*.

## Awareness vs. "Self-Awareness"

To be a Grownup, you have to live in the Real World. You not only have to live in the Real World, but you have to have an accurate picture of how it works. This automatically excludes every student and every teacher on every college campus in the world. (For reasons why school is not the Real World, see "Striking Similarities Between College and the Womb."

The Real World (also known as Life) is tough. You get junk mail. You have to buy groceries. You have to pay your parking tickets, or they'll tow away your car and make you pay double before you get it out. In the Real World, you get back to basics: what matters isn't beers, books, and dorm blasts, but food, clothing, and shelter—all of which must be bought and paid for; you have to have a job.

Mere Adults would rather not deal with the Real World, preferring instead to dwell on the "inner self" as the best source of knowledge. This is why they choose to indulge in things like EST, primal scream, and twelve years of transactional analysis so that they can "deal" with problems they might have otherwise ignored. Not issues like Third World hunger and global poverty, but the really important problems, like:

Fear of success

Fear of being broke

Fear of getting a job

Fear of getting anywhere on time

Fear of not getting enough sleep

Fear of "relating"

Fear of *not* "relating"

Fear of therapy

Fear of being unable to pay for therapy

Fear of not having transportation on a Saturday night

Grownups are more concerned with knowing things like how to register a car, when to vote, what time the bank closes, and what to do with Form 1099. They also like to have an accurate picture of how the Real World works, and so they read the paper and watch network news and can discuss political and social issues with an acceptable degree of knowledgeability.

The same Mere Adults who can wax eloquent about their "lack of ability to commit to an interpersonal relationship" are frequently tongue-tied when it comes to the news. Grownups are patient with people like this, so long as they don't drone on.

## Responsibility vs. "Winging It"

Because it's so important to Grownups that life run as smoothly as possible, they like the people they deal with to be responsible. And why not? Grownups are responsible. Mere Adults think commitments can be broken if something better comes along. Grownups do not make commitments they do not intend to keep. (The only exceptions to this are love affairs and the stock market, where it is perfectly O.K.—and even advantageous—to change your mind as often as you like.)

Grownups are not only responsible to other people, they are responsible to themselves. They make plans and then follow through. They do not buy a *Jane Fonda Workout* videotape, put it on, and eat pizza while they watch Jane run. They do not make a list of errands and then lose the list. They do not go out for toilet paper and come home with grated cheese.

They take their vitamins, eat a full breakfast, get regular checkups, register to vote, send thank-you notes, and always R.S.V.P. Needless to say, they also get to the airport long before the plane takes off, every time they travel.

Mere Adults are sure they can always "wing it" if they're caught in a bind. This is why they never have a thermometer in the house, frequently leave the oven on, and rarely carry insurance. This is all right if they're the only ones affected by their own devil-may-care insouciance. But if they try to wing it when other people are concerned, situations like the following are bound to ensue:

Mere Adult neglects to pack the night before a trip and, naturally, oversleeps. While four people wait, he tries to put everything he'll need for a week in the Bahamas in a knapsack. He gets hysterical because he can't find his razor. Then he can't find his watch. He screams, "Go without me! Go without me!" but no one believes him. Even if they make the plane, everyone hates him for the rest of the trip.

Grownups don't like people who don't behave responsibly toward them. If they can make the sacrifice, so can everyone else.

"Keep the change."

"What do you mean, you don't take plastic?"

| THINGS GROWNUPS SAY BECAUSE THEY'RE RESPONSIBLE | THINGS MERE ADULTS SAY BECAUSE THEY'RE NOT |
|---|---|
| "Clean it before the stain sets." | "That's been there since the first time I wore it. It's blueberry jam." |
| "Do you have your keys?" | "Oops." |
| "Did we turn off the lights?" | "It's O.K. It'll keep the burglars away." |
| "Check the oil." | "What's that funny noise?" |
| "Keep the change." | "What do you mean, you don't take plastic?" |
| "I'm doing spring cleaning." | "I'm sending a lot of junk home to my parents' house. They can store it in my old room." |
| "I have to be back by two." | "I'm supposed to take an hour, but they'll never know." |
| "Let's put an ad in the paper." | "Finders keepers, losers weepers. I've always wanted a dog." |

# Discretion vs. "Asserting Yourself"

Grownups know that truth is an overrated virtue and respect other people's right to be spared it. What other people want to know is their business. This is why Grownups are discreet.

Discretion is the fine art of not seeing—or at least not commenting on—what is not supposed to be seen, like your friend's growing bald spot, his ten extra pounds, or who his wife is about to leave him for, whether he knows it or not.

Although most Mere Adults actually leave adolescence acutely inarticulate and with few opinions on anything, they are under the misguided impression that to be mature one must be "assertive" with opinions that can only be "validated" if freely expressed.

Discretion applies not only to words but to deeds. Mere Adults like to attract attention, whereas Grownups would rather do most things without a lot of fuss.

| EVENT | MOST ATTENTION A GROWNUP WOULD WANT TO ATTRACT | MOST ATTENTION A MERE ADULT WOULD WANT TO ATTRACT |
|---|---|---|
| a date | Close friend who knows; but not the details | Everybody knows; three "best" friends know the details; diary entry will eventually be published in *Cosmo* |
| a wedding | Announcement in the Sunday *New York Times* | Notice in the "Transitions" section of *Newsweek* |
| a birth | Mailed announcements in pink or blue | A full-page ad in *Variety* ("Our new production!") |
| new job | Column in the company news | Feature in *People* magazine |
| a divorce | New stationery | A parade |

This is why they will tell you things you didn't want to know and didn't ask to hear and justify doing so by claiming it's for your own good.

## WHAT MERE ADULTS WILL TELL YOU BECAUSE THEY THINK YOU OUGHT TO KNOW

Who your ex-spouse went out with right after the divorce

What they *really* think of your new beau

Why your hairstyle looks tacky

When your breath smells

When your date has had too much to drink

How your ex-lover *really* got that trip to Martinique

When you're going out with someone who's not right for you

Why you keep making the same mistakes.

# Discipline vs. "Hanging Out"

In keeping with the understanding that life must run smoothly, Grownups are disciplined. Discipline means adhering to rules of conduct. Discipline means keeping it all in. Discipline means acting like a soldier in the army of life. It's no party, but them's the breaks.

Mere Adults usually take the position that it's best to take things as they come and just "hang out." It's not always apparent at first, but hanging out eventually and inevitably leads to chaos, which is a big waste of time. We had chaos before God separated the darkness from the light. Who wants to go back to that?

Discipline, however, leads to progress. It also cuts down on those nasty surprises that creep up on Mere Adults when they've raised hanging out to an art.

## NASTY SURPRISES AND POSSIBLE CONSEQUENCES

NASTY SURPRISE NUMBER 1:

Mere Adult "forgets" to make the bed, wash the dishes, and do the laundry for weeks on end. One day he comes home to find that his house looks like it was thrown in a blender.

Possible consequence: He puts down his eyeglasses and then can't find them. He can't see at work. He gets fired from his job. He can't pay the rent. He gets evicted, and no one will take him in, because, God knows, *they* don't want him doing that to *their* house.

NASTY SURPRISE NUMBER 2:

Mere Adult goes on vacation and "pigs out." When she gets home, she figures that since she's already cheated on her diet, she might as well cheat some more. One day she wakes up to find that she can't fit into *any* of her clothes.

Possible consequence: She has to wear a raincoat to go buy new clothes. The buttons pop off. She is arrested for indecent exposure. She cannot make bail. She is given ninety days. When she gets out, she finds that she has been evicted and no one will take her in, because *they* don't want her eating all *their* food.

NASTY SURPRISE NUMBER 3:

Mere Adult has a report to finish for Monday, but it's "too nice a weekend to spend indoors." He figures he can pull an all-nighter on Sunday the way he did in college, but by Sunday at midnight he's fast asleep.

Possible consequence: Monday inevitably arrives. Mere Adult calls in sick. Boss sends a messenger over to pick up the report. Mere Adult refuses to answer the door. Boss thinks Mere Adult is a neurotic and passes him over for promotion. He eventually loses his job and can't get another one, because, God knows, people don't want a worker like *that* in *their* office.

# *Patience vs. "Going for It"*

Grownups and Mere Adults see time differently. Grownups know that anything worth getting is worth waiting an appropriate amount of time for. Since Grownups think in terms of the overall picture, five or ten years is not necessarily a long time. The same amount of time is "forever" to a Mere Adult.

WHAT GROWNUPS THINK IS WORTH WAITING
FIFTEEN MINUTES FOR

Service at McDonald's; credit-card approval (especially if they are the merchants)

WHAT IS WORTH WAITING A WEEK FOR

*Upstairs, Downstairs*

WHAT IS WORTH WAITING SIX TO EIGHT WEEKS FOR

Delivery

WHAT IS WORTH WAITING A YEAR FOR

A raise; a two-week paid vacation; pension-plan vestment

## WHAT IS WORTH WAITING TEN YEARS FOR

To have paid your dues (and we're not talking class dues)

## WHAT IS WORTH WAITING TWENTY-ONE YEARS FOR

To have made it to the top of your profession

## WHAT IS WORTH WAITING A LIFETIME FOR

Nothing. Even Grownups think a lifetime is "forever."

Fifteen minutes can be "forever" to a Mere Adult, depending on what he or she is waiting for. This can lead to impulsiveness. Of course, Grownups do not like impulsiveness, because anything done purely on impulse can lead to regret.

### EXAMPLE: THE WAITING GAME

A Grownup and a Mere Adult are in a department store, each with a friend. They realize they need some socks. Both the Grownup and the Mere Adult say, "I'll only be a minute. I'm just going to zip in and zip out." However, there happens to be a long line at the register. Here's where they diverge:

| MERE ADULT | GROWNUP |
|---|---|
| Waits. | Waits. |
| Goes to the front of the line and says, "Excuse me, can I go in front of you? I have a plane to catch." Grownup at the head doesn't buy it. Mere Adult goes to the back of the line—which is now two people longer. | Waits. |
| Waits two minutes, tapping foot, and then says, loud enough so everyone can hear and feel guilty, "Oh, this is ridiculous. I don't want them if I'm going to have to wait." No one cares. | Waits. |
| Leaves. | Waits. Two or three people make their purchases. |

MERE ADULT

Tells friend he couldn't wait "forever." Goes home grumpy and empty-handed.

GROWNUP

Tells friend there were a couple of people ahead of him. Goes home with two pairs of socks.

Of course, patience isn't easy. But it looks better to other Grownups, and it does minimize regret.

## THE "GO-FER-IT!" SYNDROME

A lot of Mere Adults are afflicted with the "Go-fer-It" syndrome. This syndrome is characterized by the indiscriminate use of the phrase "Go fer it!" in response to any of the following suggestions:

"I could really use a beer."
("Go fer it!")

"I decided to drop out of school."
("Go fer it!")

"Wanna rob a bank?"
("Go fer it!")

You have to admire the enthusiasm involved, but the attitude that anything that sounds like it might be worth having needs to be had immediately can lead to unpleasant consequences. Of course, there's a lot to be said for instant gratification. It's quick, it's easy, and you know exactly when you're going to get it. But there's a lot more to be said for patience: It doesn't make a person look like he has mush for brains.

### WHAT YOU CANNOT BE
### (AT LEAST NOT IN FRONT OF PEOPLE)

| | | |
|---|---|---|
| selfish | ungrateful | undependable |
| cranky | ungenerous | broke |
| moody | unaware | self-centered |
| irresponsible | babyish | self-absorbed |
| impatient | brattish | contemptuous |
| undisciplined | silly | lily-livered |
| totally dependent | simple | brainwashed |
| naive | messy | mollycoddled |
| neurotic | irrational | tongue-tied |
| oblivious | wimpy | absentminded |
| indiscreet | gullible | scatological |
| drugged out | reckless | hypersensitive |
| boozy | impulsive | grumpy |

In short, if you want to look like a Grownup, you must be practically perfect. At least in front of strangers.

# The Grownup at Home

As Polly Adler said, "A house is not a home." For the Mere Adult, a house is a dorm room and a home is where you go for the holidays. For the Grownup, a house *must* be a home, and there is only one way to live in it and decorate it: permanently.

## Decorating Your Home

It doesn't matter whether your taste is Danish Modern or Louis XIV. It doesn't matter if your bathrooms are done in frog motif or no motif. It doesn't even matter whether your couch is chintz or corduroy—or even covered in plastic (except when company comes). What matters is that your furniture is permanent,

sturdy, and unable to be moved without a moving van and considerable trouble. If you can fit the contents of your home in a U-Haul or the back of a friend's station wagon, *your* house is not a home.

**THE LIVING ROOM**

It is important that the room look lived-in. It should not, however, look slept in, romped in, or lion-tamed in.

Books are a pain to take anywhere, and so their presence in a home—whether or not you have any intention of reading them—is another indication of the intent to stay put. Hence, books are Grownup.

Photographs are also a must. It shows you think

The Grownup Living Room

The Mere Adult Living Room

of others—unless they are all of ex-lovers, which indicates a preoccupation with conquest and a need to show off. If this is the case, your house is not a home; it's a shrine to yourself.

One big giveaway: the pile-on stereo. This is the turntable that sits on top of the tapedeck that sits on top of the receiver, next to the one speaker that works, all piled on a board that sits on two concrete blocks. If this sounds familiar, you're not fooling anyone.

### THE BEDROOM

The Grownup bedroom must have a bed that consists of at least three heavy parts; it must be frustrating to assemble and excruciating to move. The mattress itself should be at least a double if not a queen, to sleep two when necessary. A single bed is a dead giveaway unless you live in a monastery, where you have no choice, or are a serious proponent of "the New Celibacy" and don't want to encourage yourself to cheat.

A word about what's on your wall: Anything on your wall must be framed and hung with wire and picture hooks—the kind that don't chip the plaster. Posters stuck on the wall with masking tape or thumb-tacks don't cut it. They don't give the same effect, and they're a dead giveaway, too.

### THE KITCHEN

Even if you don't cook, it is important to give the impression that you could if you wanted to. These days grown men and women have to be self-reliant. You'll need a lot of utensils, because they indicate that you are a serious cook, or could be if your life didn't revolve around your work. Try to display more pots and pans than you could ever use, some for highly specialized uses, like butter warming or crêpe flipping, and some for which even you haven't found a use. A dearth of pots and pans and utensils indicates that you eat out a lot because you can't fend for yourself. If you are on an expense account or have just moved to town, you are exonerated. If your freezer is stocked with Stouffer's, you are not.

## Grownup Books and Music

Look at your coffee table. Look next to the stereo. If your books and records don't scream Grownup, it's time to change.

When you're choosing records, singers over the age of forty are a safe bet.

Your record collection should include albums by:

| | |
|---|---|
| Ella Fitzgerald | Sarah Vaughan |
| Nana Mouskouri | Peter Allen |
| Tony Bennett | Liza Minnelli |
| Harry Nilsson | Ludwig van Beethoven |
| Dave Brubeck | Wolfgang Amadeus Mozart |
| Cleo Lane | Igor Stravinsky |
| Frank Sinatra | Gustav Mahler |
| | Stan Getz |

Other useful classics:

The original recording of *Camelot*

The soundtrack from the movie *Help!*

The Beatles' "White Album"

Vivaldi's "Four Seasons"

Stravinsky's "Rite of Spring"

Beethoven's Ninth Symphony (the one with the singing at the end)

Debussy's "La Mer" and "L'Après-midi d'un Faune" (usually and conveniently found on the same album)

A couple of Mozart violin concertos

Richard Burton reading Welsh poetry

Maria Callas singing anything

One of the things that makes Grownup music Grownup is that the people who make it are not afraid to identify themselves by their whole names. They don't make music to offend their parents. They don't make music just to show off. They are proud of what they do, and they have no reason to believe that they will not be proud of it in years to come.

Mere Adult music, on the other hand, is usually made by people who refuse to identify themselves, preferring instead to hide in a group, which everyone knows is inherently adolescent. Case in point:

| | | |
|---|---|---|
| Deep Purple | Steely Dan | America |
| Black Sabbath | The Go-Gos | Supertramp |
| Kiss | The Ramones | The Eagles |
| Queen | Human League | Squeeze |
| Pink Floyd | Toto | The Clash |

And let's not forget the Dead Kennedys and Human Sexual Response. I mean, no wonder they're ashamed.

If the changeover is too drastic for you, try some transitional music; still adolescent but made more acceptable by the fact that, although they still have funny names, the musicians all have at least two names:

| | | |
|---|---|---|
| Stevie Wonder | Smoky Robinson | Olivia Newton-John |
| Billy Joel | Gordon Lightfoot | Carly Simon |
| Joni Mitchell | Linda Ronstadt | Jean-Pierre Rampal |

## HEAVY BOOKS

When you're choosing books, go for hardcovers. They're at least 75 percent heavier than paperback books, and this makes them look very permanent. The ideal library should weigh in the neighborhood of 1,000 pounds.

Content? Oh, yes, that matters, too. Here are some suggestions:

*Passages*, by Gail Sheehy. Never mind if you haven't read it all the way through, because nobody has. This is one of the few titles you can have in paper. The fact that you have it at all indicates that you are old enough to need it.

*Maria Callas: The Woman Behind the Legend*, by Arianna Stassinopoulos. In hardcover, two pounds. This shows an interest in culture; as everyone knows, opera is for Grownups only. Mere Adults may listen to music that has words they can't understand, but not if they can't hum the tune.

*Foods of the World*, by the Editors of Time–Life. Indicates a spirit of adventure and a global perspective. Implies that you know how to cook and, obviously, that you can fend for yourself. Implies considerable discretionary income. Together all twenty-seven volumes weigh about forty pounds and take up an entire box by themselves.

*The Stories of John Cheever*. Sensitive. Intelligent. All the protagonists are over thirty-five.

*Earthly Powers*, by Anthony Burgess. A "great book" as modern novels go. Why? You need a deep and innate understanding of the inexorable inertia of life to have any idea what this book is about. Even if this book hasn't been around for a long while, you feel like *you* have, or you wouldn't be slogging through it. Heavy, obviously.

*Philosophical Explanations*, by Robert Nozick. The closest a recent philosophical treatise has gotten to the bestseller list, this book is 764 pages long, which makes it one of the heaviest books around. Have fun packing this one if you decide to move.

*The Story of Civilization*, by Will and Ariel Durant. Of course.

Anything written and signed by someone you know. If you are old enough and worldly enough to know writers who have actually been published—with the exception of Lisa Birnbach, whom everybody claims they know—you have arrived. You can get away with about ten pounds of these.

The following books can be displayed in your library, but only if they are dog-eared, yellowed, or filled with college notes. If books like this are all your library contains, it's clear that you haven't bought a serious book in years. You should update your library before you have guests.

*Our Bodies, Ourselves*, by the Boston Women's Health Collective

*Zen and the Art of Motorcycle Maintenance*, by Robert M. Pirsig

*The Preppie Handbook*, by Lisa Birnbach

*Fear and Loathing in Las Vegas*, by Hunter S. Thompson

or

*On the Road*, by Jack Kerouac

*Women in Love*, by D. H. Lawrence

*See It and Say It in French*, by Margarita Madrigal and Colette Dulac

*The Electric Kool-Aid Acid Test*, by Tom Wolfe

*The Collected Poems of T. S. Eliot*

*Even Cowgirls Get the Blues*, by Tom Robbins

*Middlemarch*, by George Eliot

*Richard Simmons' Never Say Diet*, by Richard Simmons

*Garfield Weighs In*, by Jim Davis

or

*101 Uses for a Dead Cat*, by Simon Bond*

Anything written by Sartre or Camus

---

*Unless you are a veterinarian, anything on cats is OUT.

# *Grownup Cars*

Anyone old enough to tell a Porsche from a Pontiac knows that a car is not primarily a means of transportation but a means of exhibition. A car can say more about someone—especially a man—than even his mother can. And if you want to measure someone's maturity, the car is a much more reliable source of information than the mother, any day.

CAR AS CAR

**Malibu Station Wagon**—by definition. Why buy any station wagon if you don't have at least three kids and one rambunctious dog to lug around?

**BMW**—understated and elegant; you don't need to show off, but all the other Grownups know *exactly* what it cost.

**Mercedes-Benz**—the grandaddy of Grownup cars, even without the hood ornament.

**Ford LTD**—a standard-issue auto for the no-frills Grownup, especially in brown.

**Honda Prelude**—surprising but true: Simple and unpretentious, any Honda is, despite its size, a car for Grownups, especially those who do want to get where they're going without making a statement about it.

CAR AS TOY

**Isuzu Impulse**—for people who can't tell the difference between a car and a computer game; this car is so computerized, you wonder what it needs *you* for.

**Jaguar** (any model)—the upkeep alone is so outrageous, you'd think this would be a car that only Grownups could afford. But nohhhh. People who buy Jags know what they're in for (usually split time between the owner and the shop), and what they're really saying is, "I-know-it's-going-to-be-in-the-shop-six-months-a-year-but-I'm-going-to-get-it-anyway." Very mature.

**Volkswagen Beetle**—whether you got this car in the Sixties or to remind you of the Sixties, this car is *the* symbol of an entire generation that never grew up.

**Jeep Wagoneer**—O.K., if you spend a lot of time on the beach, but does nothing for a pin-striped suit.

## You Can't Get Away With It

Grownups are concerned with what works. Mere Adults think they can get away with what looks like it works. Mere Adults think no one will notice if their pants are fastened with a safety pin, or if their shirt is missing a button, or if the lining of their coat is coming down. That's what they think.

Before a Grownup goes out in public, he or she checks to make sure that:

- There are no stains or spots on their clothes, even in the back. (Just because the wearer can't see it, doesn't mean it isn't there.)
- He doesn't have "ring around the collar."
- There are no small holes caused by joint or cigarette ashes on his clothes. (No, you can't hide them with a tie.)
- There are no runs in her pantyhose. (Grownup women carry nail polish in their handbags, just in case.)

---

## WHAT YOU USE TO FIX THINGS

| OBJECT | GROWNUP | MERE ADULT |
| --- | --- | --- |
| coat lining | a tailor | a safety pin |
| loose screw | a screwdriver | a hammer |
| shoe sole | a shoemaker | duct tape |
| eyeglass frames | an optician | a paper clip |
| upholstery | an upholsterer | duct tape |
| wobbly table | a furniture repairman | a matchbook |
| broken chair | a furniture repairman | duct tape |
| TV antenna | a repair shop | a coat hanger |
| flat tire | a mechanic | a tire iron |
| muffler | a mechanic | "Well, I'll be selling the car soon anyway." |
| curling iron | throw it out | duct tape |
| a light bulb | throw it out | throw it out |
| a husband | a marriage counselor | throw him out |

# Taking Care of Business: The Grownup at Work

Work is hard. That's why they call it work. To do it like a Grownup, you have to face some hard facts. First, forget everything you learned in school. Forget Lewis and Clark; remember Blue Cross and Blue Shield. Forget spring break; remember how many sick days you can plausibly take. Forget the infirmary; remember how much therapy is covered by insurance. Forget what you want to be when you grow up; it's too late.

Work takes place in the Real World. This is what makes it different from other life experiences, like college or the womb. And interestingly enough, there are some striking and frequently overlooked similarities between college and the womb.

---

**WHAT COLLEGE AND THE WOMB HAVE IN COMMON**

1. You don't get paid.
2. You don't have to make your own meals.
3. Nothing you learned there means anything.

**WHAT COLLEGE AND THE WOMB DON'T HAVE IN COMMON**

1. The womb is kind of quiet. College is not.
2. In the womb there are no exams.
3. In the womb you don't have anyone borrowing your makeup or "sharing your space." (Unless you're one of the Dionne quints.)

# Do You Have a Real Job?

Since Grownups are realistic, they've reconciled ambition with ability. A Mere Adult who can't hold a bat may still dream that he's going to grow up to be a major-league baseball player, but Grownups don't delude themselves this way.

Some jobs are inherently more grownup than others, regardless of the ability involved, because they carry with them greater responsibility and therefore more respect. Or they just plain sound more grownup. Do you have a real job?

---

**A WORD ON "SELLING OUT"**

The concept of "selling out" is pure Mere Adult, and Mere Adults swear it's something they'll never do. Grownups, on the other hand, don't believe in the concept, yet they do it all the time. It's called paying one's dues.

---

| ACCEPTABLE | UNACCEPTABLE |
|---|---|
| art dealer | drug dealer |
| live-in maid | live-in boyfriend |
| stockbroker | stock boy |
| contractor | painter (especially if you wear a beret) |
| ballet dancer | topless dancer |
| cattle rustler | pool hustler |
| copywriter | songwriter |
| mail carrier | messenger |
| orthopedic surgeon | holistic medicine man |
| minister | Moonie |

| ACCEPTABLE | UNACCEPTABLE |
|---|---|
| tennis coach | tennis bum |
| weatherman | Weatherman |
| journalist | novelist (especially if you're still working on your first novel) |
| by definition, anyone who works in an office and has his or her own desk | anyone who is still working on *getting* his or her own desk |

Of course, any unacceptable job becomes acceptable if you can sell a book about your experiences.

# Getting a Job

Now, what if you don't *have* a job? You can sponge off your parents till they disown you, and then you can go live with your friends till they kick you out. But before you've lost them all, it's probably a good idea to get some work of your own.

First, send out some résumés. Here you have a choice. You can either send one out that shrieks, "No! I've never been meaningfully employed in my life and wouldn't know a job if it danced the polka on my front lawn!!" Or you can send out a résumé that looks grownup.

Here are two samples:

## THE RÉSUMÉ THAT GIVES YOU AWAY

Betsy "Bits" Carson

| | |
|---|---|
| Permanent Address: | Current Address |
| (parents) | (Until June 1984) |
| 267 Water Street | Lowell House A-32 |
| Providence, R.I. 02198 | Cambridge, Mass. 02138 |

Education:

Harvard University. Cambridge, Mass. B.A. English and American Literature (June 1984). Minor Field: Government. Activities: Drama Club II, III, IV. Varsity Field Hockey I, II.

Hope High School. Providence, R.I. 1980. Curriculum included English, History, Math (Algebra and Geometry), French, Biology, and Chemistry. Activities: French Club I, II, III, IV. Field Hockey III, IV.

**Work Experience:**

Summer:  Intern. Senator Claiborne Pell's office, Washington, D.C. My job included research and office work and a special project on congressional spending. I was one of six female interns on Capitol Hill. June-September 1983.

Salesgirl. Bloomingdale's, N.Y. (Designer Shoes) June-September 1982.

Salesgirl. Jordan Marsh, R.I. July 1981.

Part-time:  Loeb Drama Center Box Office. Cambridge,Mass. February-June 1984. My job includes phone sales and handling subscriptions.

Head Usher. Loeb Drama Center. Cambridge, Mass. My job included briefing other ushers, and audience management. September 1982-June 1983.

Harvard Alumni Office. Cambridge, Mass. Filing, typing, and general office work. September 1981-June 1982.

Miscellaneous:  Experimental Theater Class. First semester of my senior year in high school, I taught an experimental theater class consisting of ten students where I directed scenes from "Story Theatre." I did not get paid.


**References:**
Professor James McCalister
c/o English Department, Harvard University.


Personal Assessment: Has verve, self-confidence, and the ability to handle most tough situations. I also have a good head on my shoulders and feel that I am up to any job.

# THE RÉSUMÉ THAT WORKS

John B. Fasttrack

*Even if you don't have a middle initial, make one up.*

149 E 75th Street #7B
New York, NY 10014

## EDUCATION

M.B.A. June 1984 <u>Harvard Business School</u>

B.A. June 1980 { <u>University of Maryland</u> Majored in Engineering and Applied Sciences with specialization in Applied Mechanics. Significant course work in computer programming and graphic design.

*No-nonsense major*

## WORK EXPERIENCE

June–Sept. 1983     T. J. Holt and Co.     Westport, Connecticut
Investment and securities advisory firm. Consultant. Analyzed results of investor's survey and wrote a major portion of the pamphlet, "Investments for the 80's."

Sept. 1980–June 1982     Fasttrack Inc.     Washington, D.C.
President. Started and managed own transportation company, specializing in limousine service for high-ranking diplomats and VIPs. Billed over $40,000 a year.

*So what if it's his own firm? Title still impresses*

*The dollar figure is unimpressive, but "billed over" makes it sound better.*

June–Sept. 1980     Going Places Travel Bureau     Baltimore, Maryland
Consultant. Analyzed vacation patterns and packaged educational tours for business people. Job included extensive North American travel.

Sept. 1979–May 1980     University of Maryland     College Park, Maryland
Director of the Shuttle Bus Service. Supervised the operation of

transportation service for handicapped persons. 30 employees. 4 vehicles.

*Good use of college major.*

| | | |
|---|---|---|
| June–Sept. 1979 | Department of Public Works | Baltimore, Maryland |

Systems Analyst, Computer Programmer, Administration Section. Compiled performance and cost studies of targeted divisions and programmed and implemented computer projects in this 72-vehicle operation.

*They must have liked him*

| | | |
|---|---|---|
| June–Sept. 1978 | Department of Public Works | Baltimore, Maryland |

Civil Engineer's Aide, Engineering Section. Performed all office functions including drafting, surveying, computer programming, and cost studies.

## SKILLS

Civil and industrial drafting.
Computer Programming in the BASIC, FORTRAN, COBOL, and PPL languages.
Auto mechanic, self-taught.

## INTERESTS

*Implies he's broad-minded. Applies to any job.*

Travel.

## REFERENCES

Available on request.

*Who needs references with a résumé like this? Go directly to interview.*

If the second résumé looks like yours, then you're obviously on the right—and fast—track. Whether or not you've accurately described your job experience is irrelevant. What matters is that you know what grownup job experience is and you've had some contact with it.

You've faked your way into the interview. To get the job, all you have to do is dress the part.

41

# Business Dress

Appearances count. Grownups dress for the interview as if they've already got the job. Notice the difference between the Grownup and the Mere Adult conception of "the Work Look."

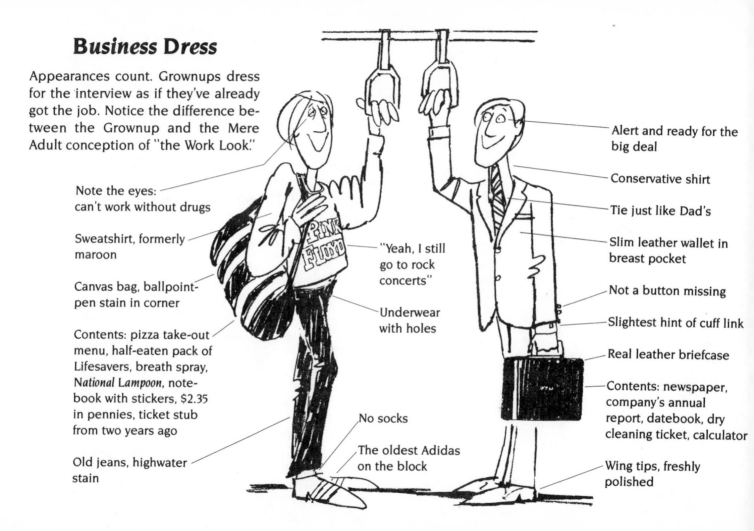

Note the eyes: can't work without drugs

Sweatshirt, formerly maroon

Canvas bag, ballpoint-pen stain in corner

Contents: pizza take-out menu, half-eaten pack of Lifesavers, breath spray, *National Lampoon*, note-book with stickers, $2.35 in pennies, ticket stub from two years ago

Old jeans, highwater stain

"Yeah, I still go to rock concerts"

Underwear with holes

No socks

The oldest Adidas on the block

Alert and ready for the big deal

Conservative shirt

Tie just like Dad's

Slim leather wallet in breast pocket

Not a button missing

Slightest hint of cuff link

Real leather briefcase

Contents: newspaper, company's annual report, datebook, dry cleaning ticket, calculator

Wing tips, freshly polished

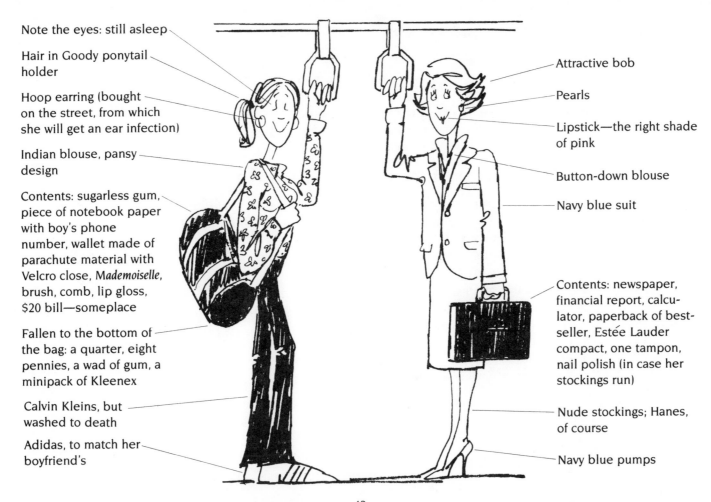

Note the eyes: still asleep

Hair in Goody ponytail holder

Hoop earring (bought on the street, from which she will get an ear infection)

Indian blouse, pansy design

Contents: sugarless gum, piece of notebook paper with boy's phone number, wallet made of parachute material with Velcro close, *Mademoiselle*, brush, comb, lip gloss, $20 bill—someplace

Fallen to the bottom of the bag: a quarter, eight pennies, a wad of gum, a minipack of Kleenex

Calvin Kleins, but washed to death

Adidas, to match her boyfriend's

Attractive bob

Pearls

Lipstick—the right shade of pink

Button-down blouse

Navy blue suit

Contents: newspaper, financial report, calculator, paperback of best-seller, Estée Lauder compact, one tampon, nail polish (in case her stockings run)

Nude stockings; Hanes, of course

Navy blue pumps

# *Signing Your Name*

Your signature is a very private thing, and only you should be able to read it. If any of the letters in your name can still be made out by anyone other than a trained graphologist, try this technique:

## SEVEN STEPS TO A RESPECTABLE SIGNATURE

1. Put a pad of paper on a pillow, and put the pillow on your lap.
2. Now write your name two hundred times without stopping and without any space between any of the letters. *Don't separate any letters.* Press as hard as you can and don't give up. Pretty soon you'll notice that your signature looks like a map of the Amazon.
3. Rest for five minutes. Get a drink of water.
4. Now measure out a four-inch piece of your handwriting sample, starting anywhere that looks good to you.
5. Cut it out with a scissors.
6. Paste it up.
7. Copy it over until it's perfect.

Next time you have to sign something, you'll have a signature no one can read. You'll be surprised at the respect you get.

# The Grownup Desk

# The Mere Adult Desk

Now let's take a look inside the drawers:

## THE GROWNUP DESK:

compartmentalized desk arranger (with stamps and
  extra supplies)
large checkbook
several rubber stamps
engraved business stationery
business cards
small bottle of Excedrin

Files:

> tax information organized by year, five years back
>   to the present
> stock reports
> files on each of the children and spouse
> vacation file (with clippings from the *Times*
>   Vacation Section, saved up over a year)

JAMES A. GRANADE, Ph. D.
1042 CEDAR FOREST CT
STONE MOUNTAIN, GA 30083

## THE MERE ADULT DESK

rubber bands
paper clips
another roll of Scotch tape
a comb
loose change (many pennies)
Dristan nasal spray
a few straws in their wrappers
a pair of chopsticks
Walkman batteries that roll around every time the
  drawer's opened
a birthday card, never sent
pink message notes (So-and-so called while you were
  out...)
*Your Erroneous Zones*, by Dr. Wayne W. Dyer
pens and pencils, many with no lead or no ink
unmarked keys—they could be for anything
confirmation of $250 pledge the Mere Adult made
  under pressure over the phone to his/her college
  fund drive
this year's tax information, which includes a couple of
  lunch receipts
a few snapshots

Files:

> What files? Everything's on the desk.

## Attitude: How to Turn Any Job Into a Performance

A Grownup can turn any job into a performance by showing the traditionally boring virtues of perseverance, patience, and simple hard work.

A Mere Adult, on the other hand, usually turns a job into a performance only when he or she doesn't want to keep the job. If they're really looking to prove their point, Mere Adults will use one of the following performance techniques:

1. Wear clogs to work because they make a lot of noise.
2. Give the supervisor the bird as soon as his back is turned.
3. Let your superiors know that *they* may need this office, but that doesn't mean you do.
4. Read the paper and put your feet up on the desk—after all, the boss does it.
5. Read the riot act anytime someone gets in your way.
6. Mimic anyone who tells you what to do.
7. Call the boss "Mein Commandant."
8. Use the office phone to make personal calls.
9. Yack all day.
10. Take a coffee break every hour on the hour.
11. Take lunch hour into next week.
12. Bring your knitting—make sure everyone knows how much progress you're making.
13. Send chain letters through the interoffice mail.
14. Use the company's letterhead to circulate fake memos.
15. Use the computer to find out everybody's salaries, including what the boss's son makes.
16. Bring your home video games to play on the office computer.

If you're a Grownup, there is only one way to leave a job—you quit.

## A Day in the Life of a Grownup

(Remember: Efficiency is the hallmark of a truly grownup day.)

7:00 A.M.  Set alarm for 7:00. Be up at 6:45 as usual.

7:05  Shave. Listen to the news. Make a note to take shirts to the hand laundry and ask for *starch* this time.

| 7:30 | Eat full breakfast (eggs, coffee, toast, milk). |
|------|------------------------------------------------|

7:45     To work. Drop shirts off on way.

8:30–noon     Work, work, work. Meeting with senior vice-president. Call exec. director re: new operational directive. "Important phone call." Check agenda for tomorrow's meeting. Confirm tonight's date. (Remind her the reservations are for 8:00, *pronto*.) Confirm reservations.

12:30     Business lunch, if all goes as planned. If not, grab sandwich at desk.

1:00–5:30     Finish up project early—deadline next week.

5:45     Health club. Add twenty pounds to bench press. Remind management about broken bench in sauna.

7:00     Cab home—change for dinner date.

8:00     Arrive at restaurant pronto.

10:00     Drop date off. Check agenda for tomorrow. Early to bed.

# A Day in the Life of a Mere Adult

7:00 A.M.     The alarm rings. Mere Adult thrashes around in bed and then hand shoots out to shut alarm off. Goes back to sleep.

7:58     Eyes open in panic. Overslept again.

7:59     Rushes to the bathroom, stumbles over junk on the floor, gets foot tangled in hair-dryer cord. Throws it in the corner, in general vicinity of dirty laundry.

8:38     Out the door.

8:41     Back to apartment to get important brief left under dining room table.

9:01     Missed the bus by thirty seconds. Banged on door. Bus driver wouldn't open it—again.

9:34     Arrives at work, makes apologies: "Alarm didn't go off."

9:57     After arranging desk, gets cup of coffee and a donut.

10:17     Finishes breakfast, leaves trash on desk, starts working.

| | |
|---|---|
| 10:17–noon | Writes two rough drafts of a rough draft. Gets sidetracked by article in Leisure section of newspaper. |
| 12:00 sharp | LUNCH! Asks co-worker if he or she wants to go out to grab a bite to eat. |
| 1:35–1:39 | Checks calendar and realizes that there is something tonight for which he still doesn't have a date; frantically goes through little black book. |
| 1:39–2:14 | Makes several phone calls. Finally someone who's not busy says she'll get back to him. |
| 2:15 | Boss comes by. Mere Adult busies himself rustling papers, knocks over the Styrofoam cup of cold coffee that's still on his desk; frantically cleans it up. |
| 4:58 | Potential date finally calls back and says she can't make it. |
| 5:00 sharp | Runs out the door and goes to a nearby bar where he hopes he'll be able to pick up a date for the night. |
| 6:18 | Finally convinces someone who's not bad-looking to go to his birthday party with him and says he'll pick her up at 8:00. The minute she's out the door on her way home to change, he spots someone better-looking and pulls the same routine on her. She also says yes and goes home to change. |
| 7:58 | While getting dressed for date #2, calls up date #1 and, in a hoarse voice, explains that he's suddenly come down with something awful. |
| 8:28 | Shows up at home of date #2. She got tired of waiting and told her roommate to tell him she went somewhere else. He goes to party alone. |
| 9:00–11:00 | Spends evening trying to pick up someone—anyone. |
| 11:30 | Goes home with her. |
| 1:18 | Makes excuses about an eight o'clock meeting, gets dressed, and leaves. Promises to call. |
| 2:03 | Rolls into own apartment, tears off clothes, drops them on the floor, and falls asleep on top of the bed. |

Every profession has unique responsibilities and unique ways to shirk them. Still, if you're going to be a Grownup, you've got to learn how to meet those responsibilities head-on.

Grownup waiters are real waiters—
*nothing* gets their attention.

## HOW TO BE A GROWNUP...

### ...WAITER

Take it seriously. This is a career, not a job you take to pay for your acting classes. So don't get cute with the customers. This career is a pain in the neck, but a Grownup doesn't go into it with illusions. The bright side is that since there aren't many real waiters, chances are you'll still be working long after the actors have gone home to Kansas.

### ...ACTOR

There aren't really any Grownup actors, but if you treat it as a role, you might get close. Use this excercise to prepare: Concentrate on your center, and visualize a pool of orange liquid bubbling up and over your body and enveloping you with maturity. Then imagine that liquid forming itself into a big, floppy balloon. Slowly fill that balloon with all the anger you have at your mother for not paying enough attention to you when you were first born, and the anger you have at your father for sending you to schools where nobody appreciated you, and finally, the anger you have at your shrink for not understanding you, despite years of therapy. Then let the balloon just float away, taking with it all the anger you have at the entire world for not seeing that you are the center of it. Open your eyes. You are ready to step into your role.

## …HIGH SCHOOL TEACHER

Make it clear who is in control by grading papers as if you were running a reeducation center in South Vietnam. Don't let your students get away with anything. Let them know you are on to their lack of dedication to the subject by writing nasty, one-word comments in the margins, like "Source?" "Grammar?" Don't forget the question mark at the end of every comment, to indicate that you may in fact be wrong, but you don't think so.

## …ROCK STAR

Forget it.

## …GRADUATE STUDENT.

If you want to be a Grownup, why are you in grad school? Get a job!

## …DOPE PEDDLER

Your ambition should be to advance beyond a "hands-on" position to the role of middleman. Learn how to structure deals, and pick up as many political pointers as you can along the way. Make a lot of money, invest it wisely, and get out as soon as you've made enough to pay for business school.

## …BANK TELLER

Treat customers as if it's your money to lend. Make them think that you're getting them out of a tough financial bind, but you don't want them to forget that you're doing them a favor. Count, double count, then count again, so they'll be sure that you know *exactly* how much money you've given them, in case you ever want it back. Remember: They have to come to you. You don't have to go anyplace. You don't even need them.

## …BANKER

All bankers are, by definition, grownup.

...DOCTOR

Everyone realizes the Messiah's not coming, so why shouldn't you step into the void? Who's going to challenge you for it? A lawyer?

...ENTREPRENEUR

You only need four things: (1) the ability to turn ideas into concepts, (2) the ability to turn concepts into plans, (3) the ability to turn plans into strategies, and (4) the ability to confuse other people into investing in your ideas.

...PSYCHIATRIST

Grownup psychiatrists know that their role is to solve problems, not to make them worse. Just remember: Your patients are not there to solve *your* problems; you're there to solve theirs.

## Taxes and Other Traumas

Any person who actually pays the government 60 percent of his or her income in taxes is not a Grownup, just a rich Mere Adult. Grownups know about and use shelters, loopholes, dubious but legal deductions, and a tax accountant to equal things out. The only exceptions are politicians, who have to make full disclosures of their financial situations to serve as examples for everyone else. But why follow their example?

For the Grownup taxpayer, the most traumatic questions on a tax return are:

What is your name?

and

What is your current address?

Trust your accountant with the rest.

# The Grownup at Play

Mere Adults play hard and think they have all the time in the world to do it. Grownups work hard and enjoy themselves during "leisure time," which takes place for several hours every evening, on weekends when they don't have to visit relatives, and during their two-week vacation every year. Grownups take leisure time as seriously as they take work, for they know that it must be earned. But, like anything worth working for, it's highly rewarding.

If the necessary precautions are not taken, however, leisure time can become dangerous. A single evening is not usually long enough to be a threat, but during the seemingly harmless two-day period known as the weekend, a person who is in every other way a Grownup can slip back into Mere Adulthood for twelve, twenty-four, even forty-eight hours and face a severe identity crisis on Monday morning.

## The Weekend

A typical Mere Adult weekend—the result of a cavalier attitude toward planning—goes something like this:

Friday night, cruise over to a party, get smashed, roll home, sleep through Saturday morning, wake up with a hangover, mosey to the kitchen for breakfast at noon, mosey around the house, catch some TV, hang out with amigos, catch a movie, go to a bar, get smashed, roll home, sleep through Sunday morning, wake up with a hangover, mosey to the kitchen for breakfast at noon, glance at the paper, mosey around the house, catch some TV, call up some friends, mosey over to their house, mosey home, catch "60 Minutes," fall asleep in front of the tube, wake up Monday ... Can't wait for next weekend.

Grownups are aware that leisure time is in limited supply and are therefore careful not to squander it. *They* know that you can't underestimate the importance of planning.

A typical plan for a Grownup weekend goes something like this:

A. Friday night
   1. Quick drink after work.
   2. Pick up suit before seven for party on Saturday.
   3. Watch "MacNeil-Lehrer Report."
   4. Dinner with Harriet.

B. Saturday day
   1. Sleep until ten.
   2. Organize drawers and shelves.
   3. Jog five miles.
   4. Lunch with Steve.
   5. Sit in park, if nice.
   6. 4:45 movie.

C. Saturday night
   1. Dinner party at Mike and Sheila's.

D. Sunday
   1. Read the paper.
   2. Brunch with Tim, Sue, Lisa, and Mark.
   3. Free time.
   4. Prepare project for Monday.
   5. Call Mike and Sheila to thank them for the party.

# Parties

The purpose of a Mere Adult party is to get all your friends together to get smashed or stoned and exchange unintelligent comments that can hardly be heard over "the tunes." The purpose of a Grownup party is to obligate your friends to invite you to parties at their houses. This is why Grownup and Mere Adult parties hardly resemble each other at all.

## MERE ADULT

**Planning:** Takes two to four hours.

**Four hours before:** The roommates decide to have a party.

**Two hours before:** They decide to call people.

**One hour before:** They decide to clean up and push the furniture against a wall. They decide to empty the garbage.

**Forty-five minutes later:** They call everyone back to say it's BYOB. And bring friends.

**8:00:** Someone goes out to get beer, just in case.

**8:15:** Someone goes out to get Ruffles and Lipton onion soup and sour cream. For fifteen minutes, no one's home.

**8:30:** First guests arrive, claiming they couldn't find a liquor store that was open.

**9:00:** Other people arrive, bringing people the hosts have never seen before, many claiming they couldn't find a liquor store that was open.

**9:30:** Ruffles run out. Someone is sent out to buy more beer.

## GROWNUP

**Planning:** Takes two to four weeks.

**Four hours before:** Maid finishes vacuuming and goes home.

**Two hours before:** Caterer arrives.

**One hour before:** Bartender arrives; hostess gives instructions and then goes upstairs to get dressed.

**Forty-five minutes later:** Hostess asks host when he's planning on getting dressed.

**8:00:** Host tries to get into the bathroom to shave.

**8:15:** First guests arrive. Hostess greets them. Tells them host will be down in a minute. He's upstairs in his underwear.

**8:30:** Most of the other guests arrive. Hostess runs into kitchen to make sure hors d'oeuvres are being heated.

**9:00:** Hostess runs into kitchen to make sure dinner is being heated.

**9:30:** Dinner is served. In the dining room.

**10:30:** Neighbors complain about the noise.

**11:00:** People start dancing. Music gets turned up.

**11:30:** Neighbors threaten to call the police if music isn't turned down.

**12:00:** The police come.

**12:30:** More guests come.

**1:00:** Music gets turned up.

**1:30:** Neighbors threaten to have them evicted if they don't turn the music down.

**2:00:** Ten people leave and go to the International House of Pancakes.

**2:30:** The remaining guests get stoned.

**3:30:** The hosts go to bed. Some people go home. Someone passes out on the couch.

**4:45:** One of the roommates trips over a beer can on his way to the bathroom and wakes everyone up. Stragglers go home.

**10:30:** Hostess runs into kitchen to make sure dessert is *not* being heated.

**11:00:** Everyone moves into the living room for coffee and after-dinner liqueur.

**11:30:** Lively conversation. The caterers clean up.

**12:00:** The host tips the help.

**12:30:** Everyone leaves.

**1:00:** Host and hostess have a quiet drink together and figure out how many parties their friends owe them now.

**1:30:** Host and hostess turn in.

# Grownups and the Cinema

Others may see movies. Grownups see "films."

What is a film? Anything foreign. Anything with a message, especially one that isn't funny. Anything with more talking than action. And, of course, anything that has ever appeared on a syllabus for Film Aesthetics 101.

And a movie? Anything entertaining, easy to understand, and guaranteed not to provoke a political argument between you and your date, thereby ruining your chances of ending up in bed later on.

The acid test, of course, is popcorn. You are *supposed* to eat popcorn at a movie. You should feel *stupid* eating popcorn at a film.

| FILMS | MOVIES |
|---|---|
| *Women in Love* | *Women in Chains* |
| *Rules of the Game* | *Everything You've Ever Wanted to Know About Sex* |
| *Seven Beauties* | *Seven Brides for Seven Brothers* |
| *8½* | *10* |
| *Claire's Knee* | *Deep Throat* |
| *La Dolce Vita* | *Marriage, Italian Style* |
| *The Marriage of Maria Braun* | *Divorce, Italian Style* |
| *The Seventh Seal* | *One Hundred and One Dalmations* |
| *Cries and Whispers* | *Scream Bloody Murder* |
| *My Dinner with André* | *Diner* |
| Anything by Ingmar Bergman (no matter how hard he tries to be entertaining) | Anything by Woody Allen (no matter how hard he tries to be Ingmar Bergman) |

There are some movies that are also films. They have Humphrey Bogart and/or Ingrid Bergman in them, or they were made by Alfred Hitchcock or Orson Welles. If you are a Grownup, you will refer to them as "films"—often and always—despite the fact that you enjoy them and actually understand what they're about.

A real film, however, concerns a bad experience, and if it is a serious film, it should be a bad experience for you as well. True, you won't enjoy it, but you will appreciate it. After all, learning from experience is what growing up is all about.

# Vacations and Vacation Spots

| YES | NO |
|---|---|
| A cabin in Vermont that your family's had for years | A cabin in the Poconos where 178 couples have sipped champagne in the heart-shaped bathtub before you |
| The Hamptons—as long as it's not a share | The Hamptons—especially if it is a share |
| Club Med for couples | Club Med for singles |
| The Golden Door in Phoenix | The Golden Nugget in Las Vegas |
| A week-long barge trip down the Seine (wine-tasting expedition) | A weekend on a boat tied to a pier (alcohol-tolerance experiment) |
| Winter vacation in Bermuda | Spring break in Fort Lauderdale |
| All winter in Miami Beach | All summer at Rehoboth Beach |
| A jungle safari in Swaziland | The Jungle Ride at Disneyland |
| Tennis camp (where you'll perfect your backhand technique) | Computer camp (where you'll perfect your Pac-Man technique) |

YES: A weekend in bed

NO: A weekend at your grandparents'

# How to Handle the Holidays

Holidays are the times when you are involuntarily thrown together with members of your family who want to bug you mercilessly until they find out exactly where you stand on the developmental scale. So think of the holidays as a test; be prepared for short answer, multiple choice, as well as essays. And if anyone tells you there are no right answers, they're just trying to mess you up.

### SAMPLE HOLIDAY ACHIEVEMENT TEST, OR S.H.A.T.

The following are questions you're likely to hear and some possible answers:

1. "Do you have a boyfriend now?"

    UNACCEPTABLE ANSWERS:

    "Frankly, I prefer casual sex."

    "I'm really not into men, if you follow my drift."

    "Get off my case."

    THE CORRECT RESPONSE IS:

    "I see quite a bit of one fellow. You'd like him a lot."

2. "So, when are you getting married?"

    UNACCEPTABLE ANSWERS:

    "When hell freezes over."

    "Awww, Mom…"

    "Get off my case."

    THE CORRECT RESPONSE IS:

    "Now what kind of a question is that?"

3. "Your sister looks awful. Do you know why?"

    UNACCEPTABLE ANSWERS:

    "No. Should I?"

    "She looks the same to me—bad. Har, har."

    "She's dating a coke dealer. I'd be shocked if she got any sleep."

    THE CORRECT RESPONSE IS:

    "I was just noticing that myself. Maybe we should have a talk with Mother."

4. "Have you lost a lot of weight?"

    UNACCEPTABLE ANSWERS:

    "I'm on this great diet—all I eat is grapes."

    "No. I just left it some place."

    "It's not from clean living—if you know what I mean."

    THE CORRECT RESPONSE IS:

    "Yes. Thank you."

5. "Do you think your mother needs help?"
   UNACCEPTABLE ANSWERS:
      "She sure does. Yuk, yuk."
      "I tell her every year not to invite the relatives."
      "Let her work. It's good for her."
   THE CORRECT RESPONSE IS:
      "Mother, can we help?"

6. "Sounds like you have some problems. Have you thought about getting help?"
   UNACCEPTABLE ANSWERS:
      "No. Have you?"
      "You mean, like a maid?"
      "I don't believe in that shit."
   THE CORRECT RESPONSE IS:
      "Get off my case."

---

## THANKSGIVING—THE BARE NECESSITIES

| CHILD | MERE ADULT | GROWNUP |
|---|---|---|
| Turkey | Turkey | Turkey |
| Stuffing | Stuffing | Stuffing |
| Children's table in the kitchen | Matching plates | The good silver |
| Family, including several cousins and siblings your own age | Family, including parents you're trying to convince you're old enough to make your own decisions | The in-laws |
| A temper tantrum at the table over who got thirds. Everyone gets cranky. | A loud argument in the kitchen over which spices to put in the pumpkin pie. Everyone gets hungry. | A disagreement over politics that will develop into a loud argument over drinks and continue at the table between clenched teeth. Everyone gets soused. |

## CHRISTMAS

| CHILD | MERE ADULT | GROWNUP |
| --- | --- | --- |
| A tree | A tree | A tree |
| Decorations you made yourself out of construction paper, macaroni, and gold spray paint | Decorations you have to replace every year because you break them | Decorations you use every year because they've been handed down |
| Some presents that were just what you asked for | Some presents that were just what you asked for | Some children |
| Some presents that were not what you wanted at all | Some presents that were almost what you asked for, except they're the wrong color and size | Some relatives who give you the same gift every year |
| A temper tantrum over the presents that were not what you wanted at all | A loud argument over the insensitivity of some people who *still* don't know you've outgrown pink | A continuation of the argument you were having the last time |

# Choosing the Appropriate Gift

There are many occasions on which the giving of a gift is in order. Mere Adults think that they are only obligated to shell out for three: birthdays, holidays, and Mother's Day. (A card usually suffices for Father's Day.)

Grownups know that they may be expected to cough up presents for all sorts of other trumped-up occasions as well: housewarmings, graduations, anniversaries, weddings, baby showers, going-away parties, retirements, Secretary's Day. Almost any occasion is fair game, and the Grownup is a sitting duck.

Because Grownups are continually vulnerable to these sorts of occasions, they have an ingrained awareness of which presents are appropriate for which recipients. Their job is simplified by the fact that there are really only two basic gift groups: Toys and Clothes. For a child, Toys are toys and Clothes are clothes. For a Mere Adult, Toys are drugs and Clothes are books. For a Grownup, Toys are clothes and Clothes are anything for the house.

## GROWNUP-TO-GROWNUP GIFTS

TOYS

A fur coat

A Rolex watch

A nine iron

Symphony tickets

A year's subscription to the *New Yorker*

An Elizabeth Arden "Miracle Morning"

A good bottle of wine

A bottle of wine that looks better than it really is

CLOTHES

A brass umbrella stand shaped like a Spanish boot

A Buddha with a clock in its stomach

An automatic coffee-bean grinder

A set of jumper cables

Sheepskin car-seat covers

A battery-run miniature car vacuum

Anything monogrammed (like boxer shorts given by a woman to a man, monogrammed with *her* initials)

Anything you got for your last birthday and didn't want

A ten-speed blender

A new refrigerator with an ice-and-water dispenser on the door

A washer/dryer with a buzzer that goes off when your clothes are done

First session at the shrink's

## MERE ADULT-TO-MERE ADULT GIFTS

A gram of cocaine and a couple of 'ludes

A "fuzz buster" (antiradar device)

A year's subscription to *People* magazine

A T-shirt emblazoned with one of the following:
"Stop Staring at My Chest!"
"My Best Friend Went to New York, and All She Got Me Was This Lousy T-Shirt!"
"I'm Not Easy, I'm Just Horny as Hell"

Two scented candles (the fat ones)

A record—any record

A humorous book, like *Titters 101*, or *The Preppie Handbook*

# Grownup Vices

The difference between Grownup vices and kids' vices is that Grownup vices cost more.

| KIDS' VICES | GROWNUP VICES |
|---|---|
| Kissing on the first date | Kissing before the first date |
| Going all the way with someone you've only known a couple of weeks | Going home with a couple you've only known an hour |
| Playing Spin the Bottle | Playing Swap the Wife |
| Spending your entire allowance at the candy store | Spending your entire paycheck at the black-jack tables |
| Smoking cigarettes behind the house | Smoking dope behind the wheel |
| Sniffing model airplane glue | Mainlining anything that is safer up the nose |
| Smoking cigarettes when your parents aren't around | Smoking dope after your kids have gone to sleep |
| Playing baseball in front of a window | Fooling around without pulling the shades |

| KIDS' VICES | GROWNUP VICES |
|---|---|
| Dirty magazines | Whips and chains |
| Eating too much candy | Eating rich food |
| Drinking too much Boone's Farm | Drinking too much scotch |
| Barfing | Drinking |
| Mooning | Drinking |
| Fibbing | Lying |
| Staying out past curfew | Not coming home at all |

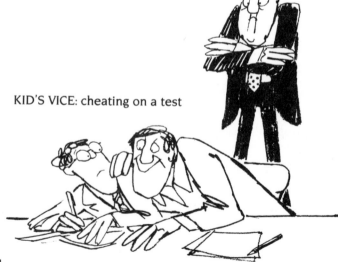

KID'S VICE: cheating on a test

# Grownup Games

Contrary to what you may think, Grownups play the same games that children play. They just call them by different names.

| KIDS' GAMES | GROWNUP NAMES |
|---|---|
| Mother May I? | Asking for a Raise |
| King of the Mountain | Climbing the Corporate Ladder |
| Red Rover | Engineering a Corporate Merger |
| Blindman's Buff | Psychoanalysis |
| Tag | Dating |
| Pin the Tail on the Donkey | Looking for Mr. Goodbar |
| Musical Chairs | Musical Beds |
| Cooties | Herpes |
| Tic-tac-toe | Heading Him Off at the Pass |
| Catch | The Wedding |
| Marbles | The Marriage |

GROWNUP VICE: cheating on your spouse

| KIDS' GAMES | GROWNUP GAMES |
|---|---|
| Connect the Dots | Figuring out why your spouse has matchbooks in his or her pockets from restaurants you've never eaten in and hotels you've never seen |
| Hide and Seek | The Affair |
| Go Fish | The Divorce |

## WHAT FASCINATES:

| KIDS | MERE ADULTS | GROWNUPS |
|---|---|---|
| the beach | the wilderness | the lawn |
| dirty pictures | one-night stands | tax shelters |
| secrets | gossip | stock tips |
| Wonder Bread | salad bars | Cuisinarts |
| beach balls | Frisbees | babies |
| finger painting | black-and-white photography | psychoanalysis |

# How to Drive a Grownup Crazy

Mere Adults spend a lot of their leisure time doing things that drive Grownups up the wall. If you want to make sure—for whatever warped reason—that no Grownups will ever think you're one of them, you can:

Ask for ketchup with your steak.

Change your order just as the waitress is bringing your food.

Put salt and pepper on food before you taste it—especially if you're a dinner guest at their home.

Bring your dog to their house without asking first.

Play with the Steuben ashtray on their desk.

Lean out a window as far as you can.

Offer to write them a check if they'll give you cash.

Breast-feed in public.

Tell them you'll meet them on a street corner—and show up forty-five minutes late.

Sit on the arm of their favorite chair.

Put out your cigarette in your food.

Leave the lights on—in their house. (After all, Grownups aren't afraid of the dark; they're afraid of electric bills.)

# Grownup to Grownup

There are two basic kinds of Grownup relationships: "Just Friends" and Romances. There is absolutely nothing worth saying about Grownup friendships, except that you should not let them mess up your other relationships.

Moving on to romances, the first thing that distinguishes them from friendships is sex.

# The Sex Time Line: Are You on Schedule?

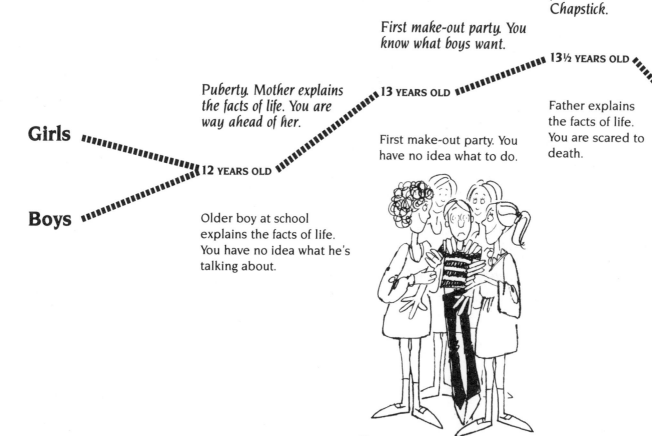

Six months of make-out parties. Nine sticks of Chapstick.

First make-out party. You know what boys want.

**13½ YEARS OLD**

Puberty. Mother explains the facts of life. You are way ahead of her.

**13 YEARS OLD**

**Girls**

First make-out party. You have no idea what to do.

Father explains the facts of life. You are scared to death.

**12 YEARS OLD**

**Boys**

Older boy at school explains the facts of life. You have no idea what he's talking about.

68

Lose your virginity to your steady boyfriend. Tell only your best friend.

Find/buy/steal a sex manual and use it to practice your technique so you'll be ready when the time comes.

Almost lose your virginity but not really. Wonder how many of your friends you should tell.

Someone you know loses her virginity. You feel very mature.

**14½ YEARS OLD**

**15 YEARS OLD**

**15½ YEARS OLD**

**16 YEARS OLD**

Someone you know loses his virginity to a girl who is 14½. You tell him about the time you lost yours, but not in detail.

Almost lose it to someone who is seventeen until she finds out you've never done it before.

Almost lose your virginity. Tell all your friends you did.

Puberty. First attempt at unhooking a bra strap. Tough but worth it.

Commit relevant parts of sex book to memory. Practice rolling grapes around your tongue without breaking the skin.

Mother casually mentions that women don't enjoy sex till they're thirty-five. You fear you may be abnormal.

**17** YEARS OLD

**16½** YEARS OLD

Everyone you know seems to be getting it but you. You try every technique you know.

Father warns you about a certain type of girl. You wonder where you can meet one.

You get the impression your mother suspects you're no longer 99 and 44/100 percent pure.

Father mentions seriously and, frequently, that boys peak around eighteen—he knows, because he was once a boy—and that you'd better watch out.

**17½** YEARS OLD

Just before graduation you lose your virginity for real. She is fifteen and seems to know what she's doing.

**18** YEARS OLD

Father mentions casually, but frequently, that boys peak around eighteen (nudge, nudge).

Your college roommate's creepy boyfriend moves in. You object, and eventually you convince her to go out with older guys.

**18½ YEARS OLD**

You move in with your first college girlfriend. Two weeks later, for no apparent reason, she throws you out.

Bump into your freshman roommate's old boyfriend and can't believe how much he's changed in two years. Start seeing him; see what your roommate saw in him.

**20 YEARS OLD**

Start seeing the roommate of your freshman girlfriend. Funny, she used to be such a bitch.

Hint to your mother over vacation that you are having sex and actually enjoy it.

**21 YEARS OLD**

Hint to your father that you are seeing a lot of someone—and actually like her.

Decide to try the New
Celibacy. Tell everybody.

**25 YEARS OLD**

Buy sexier underwear.
Hope this helps.

*Sleep around more than
you'd like to.*

**22½ TO 25 YEARS OLD**

Sleep around less than
you'd like to.

*Break up with your boy-
friend. Go to bed with
someone who's eighteen,
but make sure only your
best friend knows.*

**21½ YEARS OLD**

Break up with your girl-
friend. Go to bed with
someone who's eighteen
who thinks you're the
greatest thing since sugarless gum.

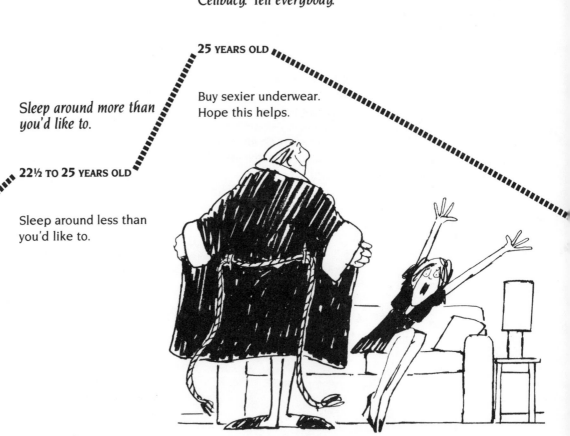

Go into therapy.

**27 ½ YEARS OLD**

Have a woman-to-woman talk with your mother about your sexual problems.

Go into singles bars.

Involuntarily start to scan the wedding announcements in the New York Times. Idly list the old friends you'd want as bridesmaids, just in case.

**27 YEARS OLD**

Have a man-to-man talk with your father about your sexual prowess.

**26 YEARS OLD**

Emerge from therapy, feeling you're finally ready to have a mature relationship.

Best man at your college roommate's wedding. Endure pointed remarks and make a note to have a serious talk with your getting-too-serious girl-friend when you get home.

**30 YEARS OLD**

Go into therapy, certain that there is no such thing as a "mature relationship."

# Sex Test

Remember the old sex test? You may have taken it when you were sixteen. It went something like this:

| HAVE YOU EVER: | POINTS |
|---|---|
| been kissed? | 1 |
| French kissed? | 2 |
| kissed lying down? | 3 |
| kissed while dancing? | 2 |
| kissed with the lights on? | 3 |
| kissed more than one person in the same day? | 4 |
| lied to your mother about kissing? | 2 |
| gone to second base? | 2 |
| gone to third base? | 3 |
| gone all the way? | 4 |
| had a hickey? | 1 |
| given a hickey? | 2 |
| displayed a hickey? | 3 |
| dated someone older (than you)? | 2 |
| touched someone below the waist? | 2 |
| let someone touch you below the waist? | 3 |
| told someone that it "won't go down unless you touch it"? | 2 |
| bought a dirty book? | 3 |
| seen a dirty movie? | 4 |

Then you added them all up and consulted the scoring system:

SCORING:
1 = pure as driven snow    2 = slightly soiled
3 = out of control    4 or more = shot to hell

The sex test for Grownups is a little different. So is the scoring.

| HAVE YOU EVER: | CIRCLE ONE: |
|---|---|
| been to a singles bar? | a  b  c |
| picked someone up at a singles bar? | a  b  c |
| been to Plato's Retreat? | a  b  c |
| picked something up at Plato's Retreat? | a  b  c |

kissed a member of your own sex?      a   b   c

kissed two or more people at the same    a   b   c
time?

cheated on your spouse?       a   b   c

cheated on your spouse more than once?   a   b   c

caught your spouse cheating on you?    a   b   c

decided to sleep around together?     a   b   c

told your psychiatrist your sexual fantasies? a   b   c

told a perfect stranger your sexual     a   b   c
fantasies?

acted out a fantasy with your psychiatrist? a   b   c

acted out everything you've ever      a   b   c
fantasized?

SCORING:
a = Yes     b = No     c = None of your business.
Add up the yeses, add up the noes; the only Grownup
answer is (c).

---

### HOW TO GET SEX THE GROWNUP WAY

Have a meaningful relationship.

---

# *Pairing Off: Grownup Couples*

When it comes to couples, Mere Adults believe that the ideal romance is one where, even if things work out, everybody dies. Examples of this are:

Heathcliff and Cathy

Romeo and Juliet

Any couple in a Harlequin romance

Grownups, on the other hand, realize that, even if things don't work out, everybody lives. Examples of this are:

Martha and George (*Who's Afraid of Virginia Woolf?*)

Eleanor of Aquitaine and Henry II

Any couple in a John Updike novel

Although it is necessary to pass through the Mere Adult stage, Grownups don't wallow in it any more. First of all, the "romance by death" syndrome is nonproductive in the extreme. Second, it is not a good model on which to base one's own relationships. And third, believing that if things work out and you are actually stuck in a real relationship you can always die shows a marked aversion to commitment.

## OTHER GROWNUP COUPLES

Paul Newman and Joanne Woodward
Cliff Robertson and Dina Merrill
William F. Buckley and Pat Buckley
Queen Elizabeth and Prince Philip

## COUPLES WHO NEVER MADE IT

Liz Taylor and Eddie Fisher
Liz Taylor and Richard Burton
Liz Taylor and John Warner
Liz Taylor and Victor Luna and Richard Burton
Elton John and Divine

# Clip and Save

## HOW TO ASK FOR A DATE

1. Find a phone.
2. Dial the correct number.
3. If the intended date answers, skip to step 6.
4. If her roommate answers, *do not hang up.* Try to sound intelligent. Tell her your name, and ask if you may speak with her roommate.
5. If she says, "She's not in. I'll give her a message," leave your name and number but ask when a convenient time to call back might be. Ask her to tell her roommate that you will be calling back. *Do not ask the roommate out.*
6. When you reach the intended date, announce your name and where she might know you from. ("We met last week at the gallery opening," or "I'm responding to your ad in the *Village Voice.*")
7. If she registers recognition, tell her how much you enjoyed meeting her, or reading her ad.
8. If she indicates that she isn't entirely displeased, suggest you get together. Do *not* say, "Listen, let's get together sometime." Have something specific in mind. Coffee maybe, although you stand a better chance with tickets to a show. (A weekend in Barbados, however intriguing, is *too* specific.) *Do not suggest a roll in the hay.*

76

9. Tell her you'll pick her up on Friday at 8:00 P.M. Say good-bye. Hang up. Since you're already at a phone, you can go right back to step 2 and try for a date for Saturday.

## WHAT GROWNUPS DO ON THE FIRST DATE
### (A Step-by-Step Planner)

1. Call him and ask him out.
2. Make reservations. at a restaurant that has a wine list, which means that it serves real food (not the kind you can eat at home in front of the TV).
3. Have your secretary get tickets to the symphony.
4. Meet at your house.
5. Offer him a drink.
6. Discuss the weather and how easy it was to find a parking place.
7. Go to the concert.
8. Go to dinner.
9. Discuss the concert and current affairs—world affairs, not your own.
10. Say goodnight at a reasonable hour—after all, in the morning, you'll both have to go to work.

The Grownup date

77

## WHAT GROWNUPS AVOID ON THE FIRST DATE

Hockey games, basketball games, and wrestling matches

Drinking themselves silly

Discussing their therapists

Discussing their "inability to relate in an interpersonal relationship"

Stories about anyone either of them has had in bed

Fighting over the bill

Making out (especially in the car)

The Mere Adult date

## TO BED OR NOT TO BED?

On the first date, that *is* the question. Grownups don't. They wait till the third.

## A TEST: WHICH ONE SOUNDS MORE LIKE YOU?

Dear Helen,

Even though we talked yesterday, I wanted to drop you a note to thank you again for introducing me to Frank Morton. We had a lovely evening on Thursday. I especially enjoyed the symphony; Frank's knowledge of Mahler certainly is extensive, and he turned out to be a charming dinner partner. By the way, we went to the most adorable French restaurant—you'll have to try it sometime with Ed.

Well, enough about me. Thank you again, and I look forward to seeing you and Ed (and Frank!) again soon.

Sincerely,

LYDIA

## OR...

Dear Diary,

Boy did I meet a creep last night! I don't even want to waste space telling you about him. I'm sitting at McFarley's totally minding my own business after work, and this guy passes a napkin to me with a cartoon on it of a guy sitting at a bar with a bubble that says "Gee, I'd love to run barefoot through her hair, but I'd never have the nerve to ask!" Well, at least it's a novel approach, I think. So I look at him and he looks kind of cute for someone who looks like Jimmy Connors impersonating a frog. (O.K. He wasn't that bad.)

So we start talking, and he tells me he's a drummer and he does cartoons on the side. He offers to buy me a drink, and I say, "Hey, sure." So we have two more beers, and he asks me out for dinner. He says we'll just find a place and grab a burger.

I figure since he's paying I'll get really sloshed. Wrong. We split the bill. But when he walked me to my door, I figured, what the hey, tomorrow's a holiday.

He had to leave to jog about 7:00 A.M. But he said he'd call me soon. Hah. <u>Soon</u> is a word meaning "not unless I bump into you on the bus and it's too crowded to get away."

# Getting It

When Grownups want sex, they are either direct or discreet or, if possible, both at the same time. They do not get cute when they don't have to. Nor do they play silly games.

## PHRASES GROWNUPS USE

The direct approach:

> "I want you."
> "Let's make love."
> "Do you?"

The discreet approach:

> "I'll see you to your door."
> "Do you want to come in for a drink?"
> "My apartment's around the corner."
> "Well..." (accompanied by the appropriate gesture).
> "I don't want this evening to end."

The direct and discreet approach:

> "I don't want this evening to end. Do you?"

## PHRASES GROWNUPS AVOID

> "I'm a guy and you're a girl, right?"
> "Wanna play hide the salami?"
> "A guy's got certain needs, Marcia."
> "I'm not looking for a piece of ass. I just want to give you a back rub."

# After the Fact

Mere Adults say the most embarrassing things after sex.

If you're a man, avoid saying things like:
> "Are you O.K.?"
> "You've done this before, haven't you? I mean, a lot."
> "So how many guys *have* you slept with?"
> "So how was I? Was I the best ever? Was I?"
> "O.K. On a scale of one to ten..."
> "Where did you learn to do *that*?"
> "You didn't do this with Normie, did you?"
> "How much do I owe you?"
> "Now let's go to the videotape!"

If you're a woman, stay away from:
  "Do you really, really, really, really love me?"
  "Body by Fonda."
  "You can stop now."
  "I have this philosophy about sex..."
  "And then after Normie, there was..."
  "You don't think I'm a slut, do you?"

  "Oh, John—I mean David."
  "You were just fine. Really. Definitely in the Top Forty."

A Grownup conversation goes like this:
  "I love you."
  "I love you, too."
  "Zzzzzzzzzzzz."

## ANOTHER QUIZ

Grownups rarely find themselves in this position, but suppose you find yourself a victim of the "Mozambique Syndrome." (You wake up one morning next to someone you hadn't counted on waking up with at ten o'clock the night before and you wish you were in Mozambique.)
Do you:

(a) glance over and then hide your head under the covers, hoping you won't be recognized?

(b) dial for a cab as quietly as you can and then try to sneak out—even if it's your apartment?

(c) tap the person on the shoulder and say, "Listen, I don't really remember much about last night, but as long as we're in bed together and I don't have to be at work...?"

(d) get dressed and run out for fresh coffee, fresh croissants, and fresh flowers, and then kiss your friend good morning and suggest breakfast in bed?

As you probably realize, only (d) is an acceptable answer if you want to consider yourself a Grownup.

If you don't like coffee, are allergic to flowers, or they don't sell fresh croissants where you live, you are allowed some limited substitutions. The basic thrust, however, is still the same: Grownups make the most of their mistakes.

# Parents and Children

## Can Grownups Be Grownups with Parents?

Most parents don't realize that just because you'll always be *their* child does not mean you'll always be *a* child. This turns many otherwise grownup people into sniveling nine-year-olds when their parents are around.

How do you avoid this? There are several ways to deal with parents:

One is to whine very loudly every time they annoy you. Of course, the problem with whining "Mothuuurrrr!" or "Daddddy!" too often is that it makes you look like an idiot, especially in front of your friends. And it does nothing to change your parents' perception of you.

Another way to get your parents to treat you as an equal is to treat them the way you treat your friends. Call them by their first names. Discuss your sex life in minute detail. Ask if you can borrow their clothes. Offer to let them borrow *your* car. When your friends meet them, suggest that you all get together some night to get stoned.

These are excellent ways to write yourself out of a will.

## HOW TO GET RESPECT FROM YOUR PARENTS

Once you're a Grownup, they can no longer pull rank. So, no matter what they do, remember that you are a Grownup, just like them. Don't grimace when your mother demands to know why you don't live at home anymore. Explain that you work in New York and the commute from Boise might be rough. Don't stamp your feet when your father criticizes your hair. Ask him who cuts *his* hair, and even if he's bald, tell him you've been meaning to get yours done like his.

If this doesn't work, teach them by example. You don't want your mother to treat you like a child? Treat *her* like a child. That's right. This goes for your father too. Smile indulgently when they say something cute. Repeat it in the third person when they're in the room. ("Did you hear what they just said? Isn't that the cutest thing?") Instead of hugs and handshakes, try ruffling Dad's hair and saying, "Howya doin', sport?" Instead of making faces when Mom asks you about your love life, raise your eyebrows and tell her you hope she didn't pick that up on the street. Finally, do not refer to them as parents. Call them "the kids."

This should disorient them so much that they'll be respectful and obedient in no time.

Try reversing roles

83

## THE MEETING

Even for Grownups, the meeting between parents and lover can be traumatic. How does a Grownup ensure that all goes well?

Premeeting Checklist:
1. Brief lover on parents' jobs and interests.
2. Brief lover on parents' quirks and idiosyncracies.
3. Make sure he/she is dressed conservatively.

The Meeting:
1. Introduce your parents the same way you do your friend—first and last names. ("John, I'd like you to meet my parents, Margaret and Howard Tulip. Mom and Dad, this is John Rose.")
2. Fix them all alcoholic drinks.
3. Pray.

When your mother refers to him as "that boy," remind her that he's thirty-two and is an assistant vice-president of his firm. When your father insists that your lover's last name is unpronounceable, suggest that he better learn to do it, just in case it turns out to be yours.

Don't worry when you find yourself saying, "Mothurrrr!" If you can avoid it in this situation, you'll be the first.

# The Big Decision

It wasn't chic a decade ago. Everyone was too busy getting *un*married and rediscovering adolescence. But now that Grownuphood is back in, so is commitment. B*ig* commitment.

So how does a Grownup couple know when it's time for the big M?

1. There's no one else they want to date, separately or together.
2. They like each other's friends.
3. Their friends like each of them.
4. They can tolerate each other's families, at least once a year.
5. Their families can tolerate them together, at least once a year.
6. They don't disagree on how to squeeze the toothpaste.
7. They agree on the subject of children—to have or not to have.
8. They don't feel the need to make prenuptial agreements, "just in case."
9. They need a blender.

# Grownup Wedding No-no's

Grownups do not get married in a field, on the beach, or in Madison Square Garden. There are only three acceptable locations for the wedding ceremony: at city hall, in the home, or in a place of worship (church, temple, or mosque). Double weddings are O.K.; mass weddings are not. Double rings are O.K.; cigar bands signal a total lack of respect for the institution of marriage, as well as insensitivity to the feelings of the parents who tend to take this kind of thing seriously.

Grownups do not write their own ceremonies. They figure that if the standard cant was good enough for their parents, it's good enough for them.

STRONG SUGGESTIONS FOR A GROWNUP WEDDING

a best man

a maid of honor

at least two bridesmaids

a wedding dress that's white

something old

something new

something borrowed

something blue

NO

UNDER NO CIRCUMSTANCES

bare feet

bare chests

holy men in dashikis and turbans

rock, pop, or folk music

electric pianos

minister or rabbi neither the bride nor groom has met before

kiss that lasts more than sixty seconds

grooms who are more than three sheets to the wind

brides who are more than six months pregnant

ducking out at the last minute

THE WEDDING RECEPTION

Grownups have sit-down dinners. Mere Adults have buffets.

THE HONEYMOON

Grownups have planned honeymoons. Or they go back to the office the next day, because they are serious about their work.

# Getting Angry and Getting Even

Yes, it happens in the most Grownup of marriages. But for Grownups, the key word is *even*. It's hard not to overdo it, but Grownups are disciplined enough to know when to stop. Even if they're getting angry at the ones they love.

## RULES FOR GETTING EVEN

Don't say anything you don't want to hear repeated to you for the next fifty years.

Don't accuse anyone of anything they've never done, especially if it's something *you* do.

Don't do anything that will cost you a lot of money in penance. You don't want to make your spouse so miserable that you feel compelled to buy him or her a mink coat or a Betamax and then end up divorcing your spouse anyway.

As Yogi Berra once said, "You can't think and hit at the same time." Since you can't hit someone and expect *them* to think clearly either, don't even jab someone in the chest to make a point.

Don't take out your anger at your mother, your third-grade teacher, or your first boyfriend on your spouse because he or she happens to be around. Your spouse will eventually take out his or her anger at you on someone else, and it will start a chain reaction that could threaten the entire world.

.

## WHAT YOU CANNOT DO

Pout

Sulk

Throw things you will later regret having broken

Kick things that are harder than the foot (which you will later regret having broken)

Blame everything on your mother

This may seem to severely limit the fun you can have. However, there are a number of terribly creative and much more gratifying alternatives for expressing anger in a grownup and discreet way. You can:

Quote Shakespeare in a nasty tone of voice.

Be totally calm.

Be totally honest.

Call your lawyer.

However, the most effective way to win an argument—especially if you are arguing with a spouse—is to threaten to report him or her to the IRS. Whether or not your spouse actually has something to hide is irrelevant; you'll get a lot of pleasure watching the color drain from his face.

THINGS GROWNUPS SAY WHEN THEY'RE MAD

"I think this tells us something."

"Well…I guess you really can't help the way you are."

"I was just wondering what your shrink would say."

"I was just wondering what *my* shrink's going to say."

"Listen, you asked me to tell you when you were being rude…"

"It's not that I don't love you, it's just that…"

"When you cut me, do I not bleed?"

Compare this to:

ANGRY RETORTS FOR MERE ADULTS

"And whose fault is that?"

"I did not."

"You suck!"

"Listen, creep…"

"I'm going to count to ten…"

"I'm not going to say 'I told you so'…"

"Good. Now you know how I felt."

"By the way, your coke is shit."

# Children: The Final Step

Can you put off your next trip to Europe for twenty years? You may be ready to have a child.

## HOW TO TELL IF YOU'RE INTERESTED: THE WARNING SIGNS

Children in commercials start to look cute.

You find yourself looking in the windows of children's toy and clothing stores.

You smile at babies on the bus.

You talk to babies on the street.

When you see someone who's pregnant, you ask her when she's due.

You make lists of names, just in case.

You feel the urge to cut up someone's meat.

## HOW TO TELL IF YOU'RE READY: THE ONLY SURE SIGNAL

The child is on its way.

## BIRTH OF A CHILD

When Grownups have babies, they do it in a dignified way: in a hospital, with a doctor, and the father stays in the waiting room.

There are no:

video cameras

flashbulbs

friends in the delivery room

children in the delivery room

home births

car births

cab births

slide shows for friends afterward

Furthermore, the following is kept to a minimum:

screaming

sweating

swearing

## THE RIGHT NAME

A rose by any other name might smell as sweet, but a grownup named Junior won't ever get respect. Keep this in mind when naming your child. You don't want your child to wonder years from now what drug you were on when you named him. And you don't want to make it harder than it already is for your child to grow up.

| | |
|---|---|
| Rhonda | Chewy |
| Ginger | Renée |
| Binky | Goober |

Suzi, Traci, Staci, Mindi

(Or any other name that ends in an *i* when it should end in a *y*, especially if the *i* has a heart or a happy face where the dot should be.)

NAMES TO GO FOR

| | |
|---|---|
| Walter | Phyllis |
| Stanley | Madge |
| Herb | Shirley |
| Hubert | Eunice |
| Nelson | Bernice |
| Milton | Edna |
| Myron | Bea |

## A FINAL WORD

Enrolling in a natural-childbirth class is a very nice gesture. Most Mere Adults do it. But in the middle of childbirth, most Grownups prefer drugs. Especially the men.

## PETS AS AN ALTERNATIVE TO BABIES

Pets are an ideal alternative to babies, as long as they conform to certain rules.

## RULES

1. Grownups don't own gerbils, goldfish, hamsters, guinea pigs, monkeys, parakeets, or pet rocks. They own dogs and/or cats.
2. Dogs should not be purchased for the purpose of meeting other people with dogs.
3. Pets do not belong at the ballet or the opera. They certainly don't belong at a cocktail party unless they're just putting in an appearance before going to bed.
4. Cats don't like to be molded into interesting shapes or danced with. Cats, like babies, are not cooperative enough to be toys.

Then there are the names...

### FOR CATS

| Grownup | No |
|---|---|
| Mirage | Midgie |
| Meow Zedong | Pinky |
| Madame | Fluff |
| Maurice | Mittens |
| Midnight | Blackie |
| Silence | Paws |

### FOR DOGS

| Grownup | Only for Kids' Dogs |
|---|---|
| Count | Spot |
| Kaiser | Rover |
| Tyler | Trixie |
| Toby | Muffy |
| Hannibal | Bandit |
| Elvira | Rex |
| Roosevelt | Trigger |
| Port | Doggie |
| Hogan | Queenie |
| Anything named after a liquor, author, fictional character, or real person from your past. | Princess |
| | Duke |

### GROWNUP NAMES FOR PAIRS OF PETS

Scotch and Soda

Liz and Dick

Le Rouge et Le Noir (French for Pinkie and Blackie)

# A Day in the Life of a Child (and by Extension, a Grownup)

What you have to look forward to:

7:00 A.M.  Grownup wakes child up.

7:00–  Child dawdles over getting dressed.

7:30  Grownup yells "Are you brushing your teeth?" Child rubs toothpaste on his gums and yells back "Yes!"

7:30–
7:45  Child plays with his breakfast. Grownup tells him not to play with his food.

7:50  Grownup drives child to school.

8:00–
12:00  Child whiles away classes by drawing on the desk, passing notes, and trying to appear attentive.

12:00  Child trades lunch with other children: a bologna sandwich, milk, and a Hostess Twinkie for a peanut butter and jelly and two Cokes.

1:00–3:00  More classes.

3:00  Gets on yellow bus to go home. Grownup (bus driver) has to tell him not to "horse around" at least once.

3:40  Arrives home. Gobbles down snack Grownup has left for him and for his other siblings, ruining his appetite and provoking a fight.

4:00–
6:00  TV time. Grownup asks "Are you doing your homework?" Child turns off TV and shouts "Yes!" Turns it on again.

6:00–
7:00  Dinner, which Grownup has prepared, which child plays with.

7:00  Grownup tells child he can watch TV, but only if his homework is done. Child claims he wasn't given any homework today. Grownup is skeptical but cannot prove otherwise.

7:00–9:00  TV time.

9:01  Grownup announces "Bedtime." Child begs to stay up just one more hour, insisting his favorite show is about to begin.

9:03  Grownup wins. Child gets ready for bed. Grownup asks "Are you folding your clothes?" Child kicks them under the bed and shouts "Yes!"

9:15  Lights out. As soon as Grownup is gone, child gets up and turns the TV on again. Falls asleep in front of it. Grownup shuts it off.

# So Why Bother Being a Grownup?

It's not just the real estate. It's not just the fact that you can walk into Bloomingdale's, and when the salesperson asks "Can I help you?" you can be sure she's not keeping an eye on you to make sure you don't steal anything.

No, being a Grownup is its own reward. Grownups get treated as if they're in control of their lives, because that's the way they act. So what if some days you look in a mirror and wonder how a kid like you could be going gray? So what if you feel like you're playing dress-up every time you put on lipstick and heels? Even if you've faked your way around the board, at least you know the rules of the game. And if you fake it enough, pretty soon you'll get so good at it you'll wake up and realize that you've been acting like a Grownup for so long you've actually become one.

## THE LAST LEG UP

You know you've finally made it when:

- The waitress comes to take your order and you know what you want.

- You don't eat all your groceries the minute you get home.
- You don't let dustballs accumulate under your furniture for months.
- You have subscriptions to magazines you never even thought you'd *read*.
- You no longer think that hanging out at a bar looks cool.
- You no longer think that holding up your hair to the light and cutting off split ends while your best friend paints her nails is an acceptable way to spend a Saturday night.
- You don't need to show the picture on your driver's license to your friends; they already know what you look like.
- You can ask other people who look older than you what they do for a living, and you don't feel like you're prying.
- You have at least one major charge card that you can use to write a check.
- Your checks stop bouncing.
- You buy your own insurance.
- You pay for your own shrink.
- You pay for your own mistakes.
- You realize that your parents don't know all the answers—they don't even know half the questions.
- You think your parents are immature. You don't mind.

# Appendix

## *Grownup Answers to Mere Adult Jokes*

Q: How many Grownups does it take to screw in a light bulb?

A: One.

Knock, knock.
Who's there?
Mrs. Abrahms from across the hall. I wonder if you could turn the music down?

Q: What's the definition of the perfect lover?

A: None of your business.

Knock, knock.
Who's there?
It's Mrs. Abrahms again. We're trying to sleep. Do you think you could turn the music down?

Knock, knock.
Who's there?
Mr. Abrahms, and I want you to knock it off!
"Mr. Abrahms and I want you to knock it off" who?
Don't be smart with me, kid. There are people in this building who go to work!

# Glossary of Constantly Changing Terms

SECURITY

1. noun. A blanket
2. noun. A boyfriend
3. noun. A large money market fund

CREDIT

1. noun. As in "extra." You only get it if you answered all the other test questions right.
2. noun. As in "a line of." What they won't give you at the bank.
3. verb. You know they won't do it to your account in less than five days, no matter who you are.

HITCH

1. verb. The cheapest way to get from place to place—all you need is a thumb.
2. verb. What hillbillies do when their pants fall down.
3. noun. There's got to be one someplace, even if the deal looks great.

SUPERIOR

1. adj. The highest grade on your report card; rarely given for conduct.

2. adj. A synonym for *excellent* as in "That party was really superior."
3. noun. One of several people in your office you have to impress.

INTEREST

1. noun. As in "lack of." What you don't have when your teachers comment on your attention span.
2. noun. As in "high rate of." Why you'd rather borrow money from your friends.
3. noun. As in "controlling." What the big boys have.

FIRST CLASS

1. noun. Something you generally sleep through.
2. adj. A-1, usually followed by *jerk*.
3. adj. The way you travel when the company pays.

FORMAL

1. adj. How Grownups dress when they're wearing evening gowns and suits and ties.
2. noun. Something you wear to the prom. Comes in black, white, and powder blue.
3. adj. As in "constraints." As opposed to *substantive*.

# Who Is and Who Isn't

1. TOO IMMATURE (a partial list)

Erik Estrada
Suzanne Somers
Tanya Tucker
Tatum O'Neal
Richard Harris
Eddie Fisher
Liz Taylor
Dean Martin
Jerry Lewis
Bill Murray
Chevy Chase
Dan Aykroyd

Gilda Radner
Valerie Perrine
Madeline Kahn
Brigitte Bardot
Bo Derek
Miss Piggy
Pia Zadora
Ryan O'Neal
Farrah Fawcett
Elliott Gould
Barbra Streisand

Frank Sinatra
Andy Gibb
John Ritter
Richard Pryor
Tommy Smothers
Dicky Smothers
Tim Conway
Gary Burghoff
Dom DeLuise
Dustin Hoffman
Richard Dreyfuss

2. TOO CHILDLIKE
   Bill Murray   Mr. Rogers   Sissy Spacek
   Chevy Chase   Ruth Gordon   Mia Farrow
   Dan Aykroyd   Bette Midler   Woody Allen
   Bill Cosby

3. THE OLDEST LIVING CHILD AWARD
   George Burns

4. ACTORS WHO GREW UP
   Jane Fonda   Sally Field
   Warren Beatty  Burt Reynolds
   Robin Williams  Steve Martin

5. ACTORS WHO GREW DOWN
   Orson Welles—Corrupted by Paul Masson.
   Marlon Brando—Ruined by *Apocalypse Now*.
   Muhammad Ali—If he had any aspirations, D-CON crushed 'em dead.

6. THE KATHARINE HEPBURN AWARD FOR MATURITY
   IN THE FACE OF OVERWHELMING ODDS
   Alan Alda

# A Final Discouraging Word

It's what you learn after you know it all that counts.

—John Wooden